Skira Architecture Library

-40
The new generation
of international architecture

Edited by Zone Attive

Skira

Editor
Luca Molinari

Design
Marcello Francone

Editing
Rosanna Schiavone

Layout
Paola Ranzini

First published in Italy
in 2002 by
Skira Editore S.p.A.
Palazzo Casati Stampa
via Torino 61
20123 Milano
Italy

© 2002 Skira, Milano

Printed and bound in Italy.
First edition

ISBN 88-8491-140-0

Distributed in North
America and Latin
America by Rizzoli
International Publications,
Inc. through St. Martin's
Press, 175 Fifth Avenue,
New York, NY 10010.
Distributed elsewhere in
the world by Thames and
Hudson Ltd., 181a High
Holborn, London WC1V
7QX, United Kingdom.

Contents

7   Introduction

The awarded architects

10   Mathias Klotz
20   Bernard Khoury
30   ARO Architectural Research Office
36   CamenzindGrafensteiner AG
44   Jae Cha
48   Peter Ebner
56   Shuhei Endo
62   Jakob + MacFarlane
72   Jean-Philippe Lanoire, Sophie Courrian
80   Alfredo Paya Benedito

The classified architects

90   5+1
94   David Adjaye
98   Jesús Mª Aparicio Guisado
102   ARCHEA
106   Architectural Office Casagrande & Rintala
110   Atelier van Lieshout
114   Anna Barbara, Rachaporn Choochuey, Stefano Mirti, Akihiro Otsuka, Luca Poncellini, Andrea Volpe
118   BlueOfficeArchitecture
122   Daniel Bonilla
126   Alessandro Bucci
130   Javier Hernando Castañeda Acero, Luis Guillermo Hernández Vásquez, Carlos Mario Rodríguez Osorio, Mauricio Alberto Valencia Correa
134   Alfonso Cendron
138   Davide Cristofani, Gabriele Lelli
142   Design Office
146   Isabelle Devin, Catherine Rannou
150   dRMM
154   FIELD Consultants
158   Toni Gironés
162   Marco Graber, Thomas Pulver

166   Grego & Smolenicky
170   Greg Lynn
174   M&T, Müller & Truniger Architekten
178   Mathew & Ghosh Architects
182   njiric + njiric arhitekti
186   OCEAN north
190   Po.D
194   S&Aa
198   Sadar Vuga Arhitekti
202   Zoe Samourkas
206   Stéphane Schurdi-Levraud
210   Studio dd1479
214   Studio R&Sie.D/B:L
218   Kerstin Thompson
222   vehovar&jauslin Architektur
226   Choi Wook
230   Zoo Architects

235   Afterword

Introduction

The Prize is dedicated to designers whose works, in relation to the place where and time when they were built, have best interpreted the requirements of the contemporary world and the needs of collective living, contributing to civil and cultural growth. These are the words chosen to introduce the International Architecture Prize dedicated to Francesco Borromini, awarded, for the first time, in September 2000. They are words that highlight the cultural and moral reasons that have brought about its creation.

Clearly emerging, in fact, is the desire to place the project within the current of international initiatives that have the purpose of promoting the harmonious development of human civilisation, the values of coexistence and mutual respect, the affirmation of a structured vision of the relationship between humanity and the environment, of a widespread critical capacity with respect to progress and the transformations that mark each age of our history.

To reason around the civil value of a work of mankind, for example, means the involvement of perspectives of different formations and orientations capable, in general, of favouring the investigation of the profound reasons for a thought that is transformed into construction, carefully considering its scientific, artistic, social, cultural and technical bases.

To attempt to make a contribution to the civil and cultural growth of a collectivity involves seeking to transform the awareness of the value of works and the thought that has made them possible into widespread awareness, well beyond the limits defined by a professional environment or by the belonging to a cultural élite.

The fact that it is the city of Rome that has promoted an initiative with such characteristics is particularly significant. Reflected in the very conception of the Prize is the important moment that the city is experiencing, profoundly involved as it is in a process of planning of its own future, committed to the attempt to link an original idea of civil development with the extraordinary heritage (archaeological, historical, architectural, cultural…) that makes it unique, more open and attentive to the plurality of voices of which contemporary culture is composed.

The decision to reserve a key role for young architecture, for the most contemporary languages through which the values inspiring the Prize are expressed, broadly represents the spirit with which the Prize has been conceived and the context in which it is affirmed.

It is a choice that fully expresses the idea that a community gradually forms of itself: a conception that recognises and enhances the role of cities in the development of civilisations; that gives value to the encounters and exchange between cultures, ideas, experiences; that sees in the constitution of Europe the opportunity to give impetus to an interpretation of the world that is less ruthless and more balanced; that believes deeply in the coming together of cultures different in space and time; that seeks, anywhere in the world, innovation capable of contributing to the civil and cultural growth of our civilisations; that invests and plans to give force and perspectives to all this.

The Borromini Prize has been conceived as the culminating symbolic moment of a very ambitious, but also very complex, programme of initiatives. The story told by the images and words that follow is at the same time the successful conclusion of a journey and the beginning of a long road, still to a large extent to be explored.

Nevertheless, it is a finished, elegant story, of different possible ways of interpreting the world, the role of people and their presence in a given physical and immaterial space. A story that offers whoever wants to read it carefully many cues for reflection, for posing questions and seeking answers that transcend, broadly, the narrow confines of a vision that is only "technical", of an art-profession that so extensively involves the expertise and thoughts of human civilisations.

The awarded architects

Mathias Klotz
(Chile, 1965)

Altamira's School

Dimensions: 6.500 sq.m
Client: Public education
Place of location: Peñalolén, Santiago, Chile
Date of completion: 2000

The Mathias Klotz and architects office has worked since 1988 till today, in housing projects (Klotz House, Ugarte House, Lavados House, Úbeda House, Muller House, Reutter House, Viejo House), etc., in various industrial projects (Safex, Zofri, Entel, Wineyard Viña del Nuevo Mundo), institutional projects (Pizarras Ibericas, Altamira School), urban furniture (for the french firm JC Decaux), commercial interventions (Umbrale Shops, Metro Restaurant), exhibitions installations (X Bienal de Arquitectura en Estación Mapocho, Japanese Architecture Exhibition in the Centro de Extensión Universidad Católica), and other areas as Cinema (Last Call) and Theatre (5 Sur), as Art Director. In the moment, the office is developing housing projects in Denmark, Argentina and Chile; a circus, urban renovations, and a service building south of Chile.

Altamira's School has its origin in a competition for a 10.000 m school for 1.400 students in Santiago. It is located on the hillside of the Andes Mountains. The site is a rectangle, 60 meters by 200 meters with a 20% slope in its large side. The project is composed of four buildings, located on each side of the site, leaving a central playground that opens the view to the mountains and the city, defining an east-west sight line with a concentration of trees to the hill side and a playground over the street.

The major areas are the gym and the cafeteria which are in the centre of the site looking to the street, in order to be used for common public activities. The central volume structure is kneecapped steel, the same for supports and structural diagonals.

The roof of these spaces is an inclined surface that works as the playground of the school. The four perimeter buildings were designed to be the classrooms for pupils. The structure is made with concrete pillars and floors without exposed beams in order to have 100% flexibility.

The east and west façades are concrete, the south façade is made of wood, and the north is made of aluminium glass and coloured panels. The Altamira project is an exercise in structures and surfaces, the subject of a general proposal towards clarity and simplicity (build the borders, liberate the centre). This idea is inspired by "Japanese Park" by Oscar Prager, a project which creates an empty interior and opens the views to the mountains and the sky.

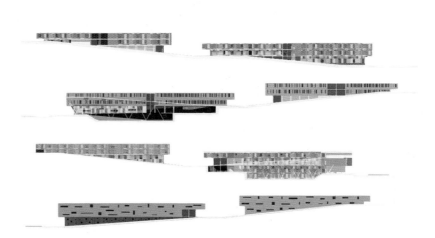

View on the main street
and of the patio

View on the courtyard

Main facades

Detail of the entrance

Detail of the portico

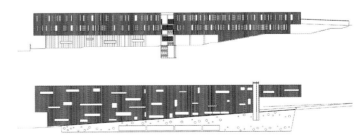

Main facades

Backfront. The gymnasium
between the classrooms
of the blocks

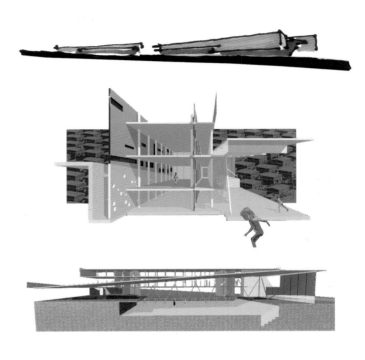

Details of the main facades

Detail of the external
platform

Ground and first floor

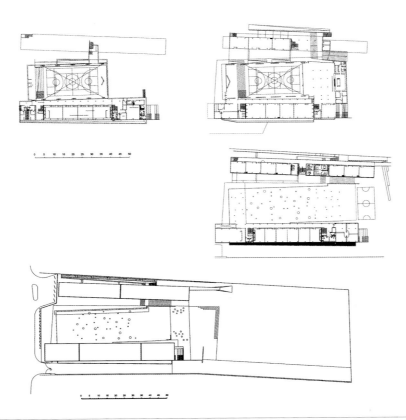

Sections

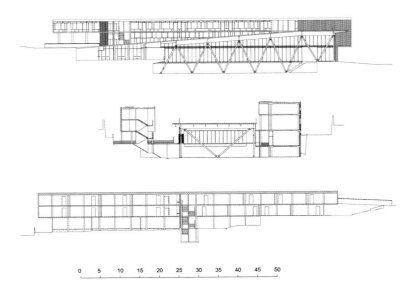

0   5   10   15   20   25   30   35   40   45   50

The gymnasium. General
views and details

Reason

I write for the purpose of nominating Mathias Klotz, specifically for the Colegio Altamira, Santiago Chile, completed April 2000. Klotz is a young architect of great promise, having synthesized international tendencies with a precise sense of place and the specificities of his own local situation. His simple formal vocabulary lets the materials speak for themselves; his restrained detailing is always appropriate to the scale and character of the building as a whole. His organizational concepts, while clear and reduced, always reflect the actual demands of the site and the program. The Colegio Altamira is his first large scale building, and shows an evident mastery of questions of form, expression and construction. The relation between the cellular organization of the classrooms, which form an enclosing block, and the large open space (open courtyard above, gymnasium below) is a brilliant and economical solution to the restricted site. Here, he makes an asset out of an apparent liability. Additionally, his solution integrates interior and exterior into a coherent whole, creating a series of transitional spaces of a hybrid interior/exterior condition. The detailing of the project merits particular comment. The precision of the steel work is set off against the intentional crudity of the concrete, reflecting the nature of the two materials, and connecting the building to its site through the roughness of the concrete, which reads as an extended ground plane. A pattern of colored panels visible through the scrim of steel mesh gives the building an optical vibration seemingly at odds with the "brutality" of the concrete frame. This montage of opposites is, I think, quite intentional, and makes the building something more than a re-statement of already known themes. It is instead a new synthesis, at once a direct and immediate index of the process of its making, and at the same time an anticipation of the complex life to unfold within the building. In the large span space below the courtyard, the structure is expressive without being overstated. Here too, Klotz exhibits the delicate strength that is becoming the hallmark of his practice. I recommend him highly.
Stan Allen

Bernard Khoury
(Lebanon, 1968)

B018

Dimensions: 370 sq.m
Client: Naji Gebrane
Place of construction: Beirut, Lebanon
Date of completion: 1998

He studied Architecture at the Rhode Island School of Design (B.F.A 1990/B. Arch 1991)
He received a Master in Architectural Studies from Harvard University in 1993.
Co-founder of "Beirut Flight Architects", his workshop is currently working on several building commissions; he is also involved in furniture design.
He is the author of several experimental projects including "Evolving Scars" issued in 1993 in the form of a proposal for the recuperation and progressive mutation of war damaged buildings in Beirut. His theoretical projects are paralleled by the attempts of their implementation and development through practical projects and building proposals. He is in charge of the conversion and several building additions for the Pfefferberg complex in Berlin.
He taught Architecture at the American University of Beirut and has lectured in several universities and prestigious academic institutions in Europe and the U.S. His work has been extensively published in numerous specialized magazines worldwide.
Khoury works and lives in Beirut and New York.

The origins: B 018 was initiated by its present manager Naji Gebrane. Gebrane is a musician; he started his professional career at the age of 12. He is co-founder of "wrong approach", an alternative jazz band. B018 was the code number of an apartment / studio situated 18 km north of Beirut. From 1984 to 1993, Gebrane lived in the unit B018. During the war years, Gebrane was famous for his "musical therapy" sessions in his B018 apartment. By the end of 1993, Gebrane moves out of his studio. He decides to take the B018 public. The first public version of B018 was built in an industrial sector of the northeast suburbs of Beirut. In its early days, B018 operated without a permit in a 200 square meter structure called the "black box"; its only access was a dirt road.

The unusual music and strange atmosphere were the main ingredients to the B018 concept, which quickly became a surprising reflection of the night scene in Beirut.

By May 1997, Gebrane was forced to leave the premises. The B018 was searching for a new address. During the closing evening of the B018, Gebrane and architect Bernard Khoury decide to build a new location for the B018. The day after, they are looking for a new site.

B 018 "la Quarantaine": architect Bernard Khoury is in charge of building the new B018, the concept of the underground structure, the scenography and furniture design…The structure was built and ready to operate in a record time of six month.

On April 18 1998 the new B018 opened its doors to the public at "la Quarantaine" lot # 317. It will remain there until the expiry date of the rental contract (November 8 2003).

The site – over exposure/confrontation: the site is located near the port of Beirut. The highway that borders the site is the main northern access to the city. This over-exposure was in certain ways incompatible with the origins of the B018. Across the highway are the densely populated quarters of the river of Beirut.

The site history – memories of the place: during the French mandate, this zone was the Quarantine of the port of Beirut, later on, it was invested by war refugees – Palestinians, Kurds and Lebanese from the southern border of the country – (about 20.000 in 1975). In January of 1976, the Phalangist militia invaded the area, the Quarantine was totally destroyed. (See photo)

The facade: the under-face of the flap portion of the roof has 126 reflecting panels on a 26s.q m surface. Seen from inside the surface reflects a descriptive section of the project, the contrasted superposition of contradictory conditions: the density of the quarters of the river of Beirut as a backdrop, the highway axis drawn by the rapid passage of the cars headlamps, the parking carousel and its lighting crown, the spectacled of the hall ended by a bird's eye view of the bar, the distortion of the reflected images is exaggerated by the fragmentation of the mirrors panels.

When opening, the roof releases sounds and light reflections, spreads the atmosphere of the place, stretches its limits, and extends its atmosphere to the outside. Its closing is a voluntary disappearance, a gesture of recess.

The roof: the structure and panels are in steel. conceived as a cap, structurally autonomous, its anchoring is imbedded under the circular concrete slab. The 5 mobile panels (one flap, four sliding) are activated by hydraulic pistons.

The loophole: located in the entrance facing the main door (dark zone), the loophole window draws itself on a black backdrop. Positioned slightly lower than eye level, it is 12 cm high by 6 m wide.

Opposite page:
Simulation of the different phases of the roof opening

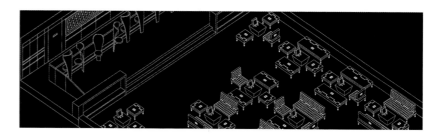

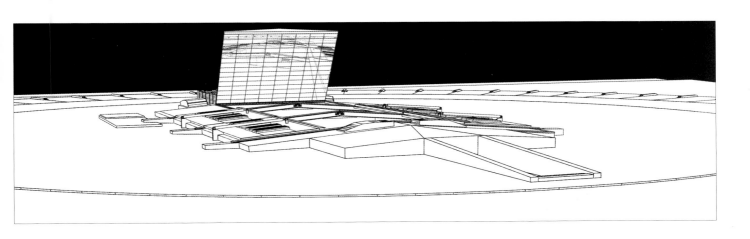

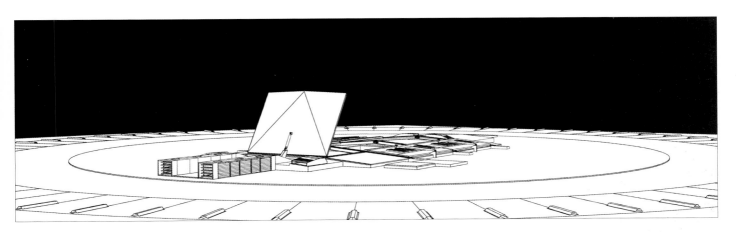

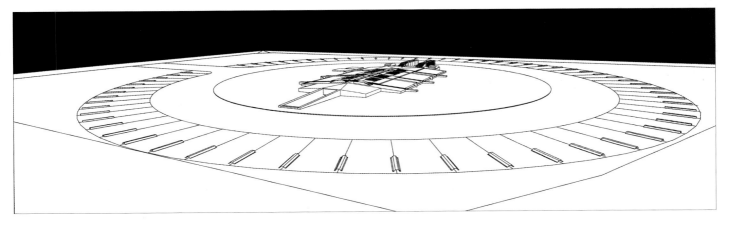

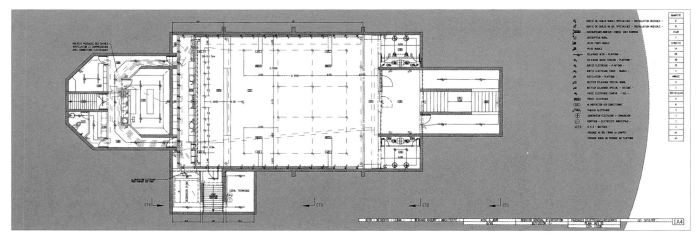

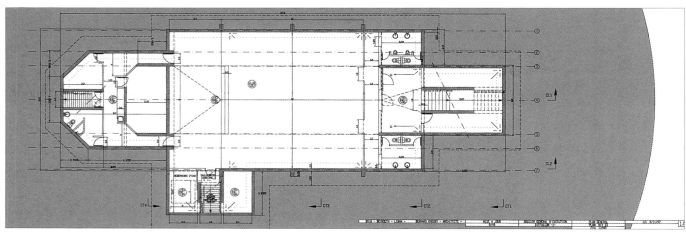

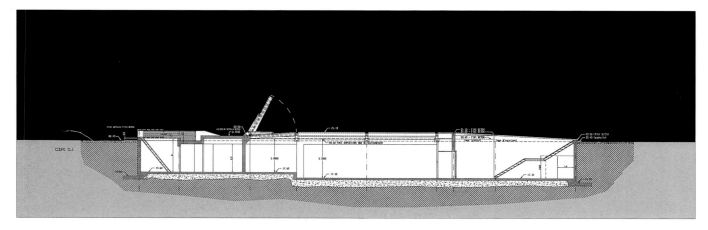

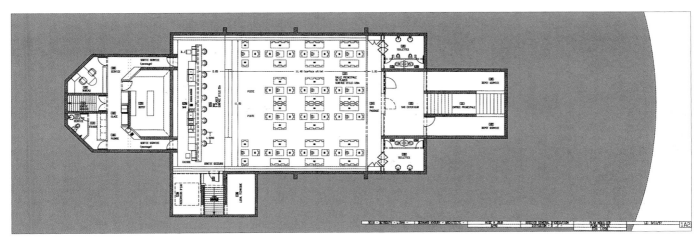

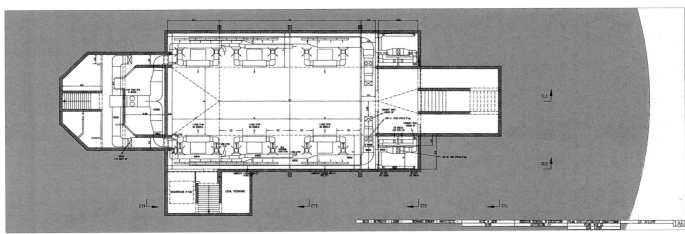

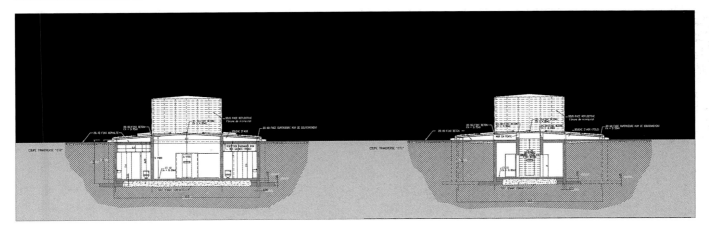

23

Details of the interiors

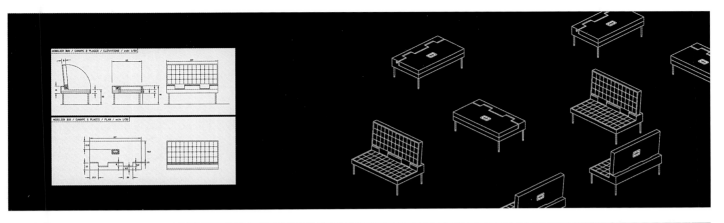

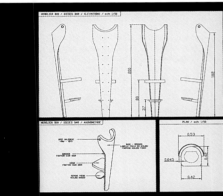

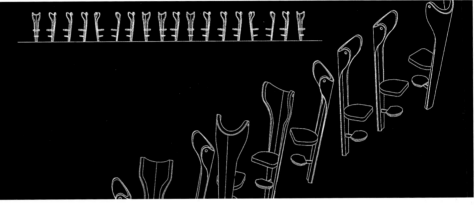

Reason

Rather than a piece of architecture, B 018 is, first of all, a tale. Naji Gebrane has been a professional musician since the age of twelve, and, among other things, the drummer of a band, whose name at that time, Wrong Approach, sounds, in retrospect, as a historical judgment on the homicidal spiral which has excruciated Lebanon since 1976. He is the initiator and the moving spirit of B 018, one of the essential places around which Beirut's night life gravitates. This obscure denomination was originally the code name of a studio located in a seaside resort eighteen kilometres north of Beirut.

Here, for nearly a decade, Naji Gebrane used to organise private sessions of "musical therapy". From 1993 to 1997, B 018 was open to a wider public. It kept its original name, even though it moved into a strange, isolated black box, at the end of a stony road, in an industrial area in the suburbs of Beirut. Equally interesting atmospheres and musical choices make the B 018 a frantic, lively place, in a city which only thinks about re-living (in all senses), whatever its price may be (again, in all senses).

A new episode, in a universe where chaos becomes a life style: 1997, B 018 is forced to move again. A place is found. Strange: an embankment on the sea, north of the city, near the port, on the edge of a highway which is one of the main roads accessing Beirut (it could not have been more visible). Radical: this place, formerly the port quarantine area, during the war was a camp for Palestinian refugees, until it was totally and cynically destroyed by the Phalangist militia, who massacred hundreds of civilians, and then left the camp to a bulldozer, something which had never been seen or heard of before (when matters become invisible, Freud no longer rules).

On top of this particularly indigestible historical millefeuille landed the third B018, the one by Bernard Khoury, first work of a twenty-nine-year-old architect. At night, bordering the highway, an enlightened concrete disc, which could have fled from Space 1999, sets the stage for the four-wheeled patrol of inveterate night-owls, whose headlights pierce and sweep the gloom. In the middle, close to a surface which is just as smooth as the urban backdrop is chaotic, metal hatches slide and open up, allowing the eye to sweep inside a pit, while music, mixed with the highway beats, comes out. Inside, their reflecting intrados distorts the city view, turning it into an urban *peep-show* subject. Below, people drink, dance, talk about *business*, kiss, show off...in a word: live. On the tables, surrounded by stand-seats which unfold like a miniature metaphor of a pocket B018, the portraits of Charlie Mingus, Serge Gainsbourg, Miles Davis, Georges Brassens, Stéphane Grappelli, Charlie Parker, John Coltrane, Stan Getz, Thelonious Monk, Billie Holiday and – of course! – Oum Khalsoum, peep and eavesdrop conversations. Through a nearly neurotic design work, which is an organic and symbiotic extension of architecture, they create a total and totalitarian manipulating object, which joyfully leads to a masochistic abandonment. *Overdesign*? Indeed, it is just in Beirut that architect Morris Lapidus, after fifteen years of fratricidal war, could have cried out his emblematic: "Too much is never enough!" Practically, it would not be surprising to find another patrol, that of Syrian guards, who, with a machine-gun by their side, come and look in from above, in the dawn light, as if on the edge of a lions' den, trying to identify the faces of these *life-addicts*, to add them to some kind of list of traitors for some kind of cause. The rental contract of this amnesic quarantine/charnel/deserted ground will expire in 2003. What next? B018 has already re-born twice: you can't have two without three. And, as far as rebirths are concerned, as well as ashes, this is a long-known tune in Beirut. *Yves Nacher*

ARO Architectural Research Office

Stephen Cassell
(USA, 1963)
Adam Yarinsky
(USA, 1962)

Established in 1993 by Stephen Cassell and Adam Yarinsky, Architecture Research Office is an eighteen-person studio with fourteen architects. We are selective about the work we undertake. Four current projects exemplify our range: We are participating in a limited competition to design a new 90,000 square-foot Museum of Art and Technology in Manhattan, with a budget of $40 million. We are preparing a design concept for an upcoming exhibition at the Guggenheim Museum. In collaboration with Rem Koolhaas, ARO is the architect of record for a 20,000-square-foot Prada store in SoHo. We are in the design phase of a $15-million, 20,000-square-foot residence in New York City. We have completed the pre-design programming phase for the $15 million, 150,000-square-foot New York headquarters of Razorfish, a "new media" company.

US Armed Forces Recruiting Station

Dimensions: 50 sq.m.
Client: Us Army Corps Of Engineers
Place of construction: New York, USA
Date of completion: 1999

The new design for the US Armed Forces Recruiting Station interprets the neon vernacular of its busy Times Square setting to establish a clear and visible presence for the United States Armed Forces. The building replaces the 1946 original and is required not to exceed its envelope. Each long facade presents itself to the passerby as an American flag made of thirteen bands of fluorescent light. Translucent reflective gels made from a material produced by 3M create red, white and blue elements that color the lights at night and reflect sunlight during the day. Specially detailed stainless steel and glass curtain walls integrate the lighting system as a whole, so that the flag lights are layered with reflections of the surrounding buildings. The Recruiting Station is a 550 square foot facility which houses a workstation for each of the four armed forces as well as a restroom, which the previous structure lacked.

The site is a traffic island between Broadway and 7th Avenue, and is outlined by reflective bollards. The entire structure was designed to sit above a functioning subway ventilation shaft. The design of the Recruiting Station was conceived to withstand a highly demanding and political review process from the client and from New York City. The flags provide a patriotic symbol for the Armed Forces, while meeting stringent zoning regulations for a minimum amount of signage. Amidst glittering advertisements and bustling traffic, the building is a stable landmark in a constantly changing urban landscape.

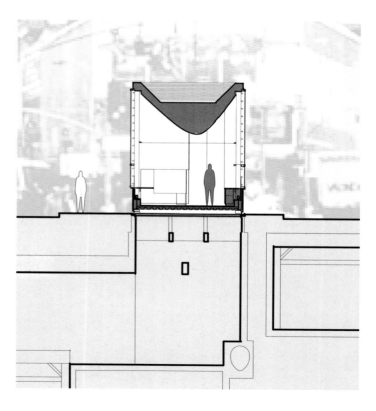

General view from Times
Square

The side facade

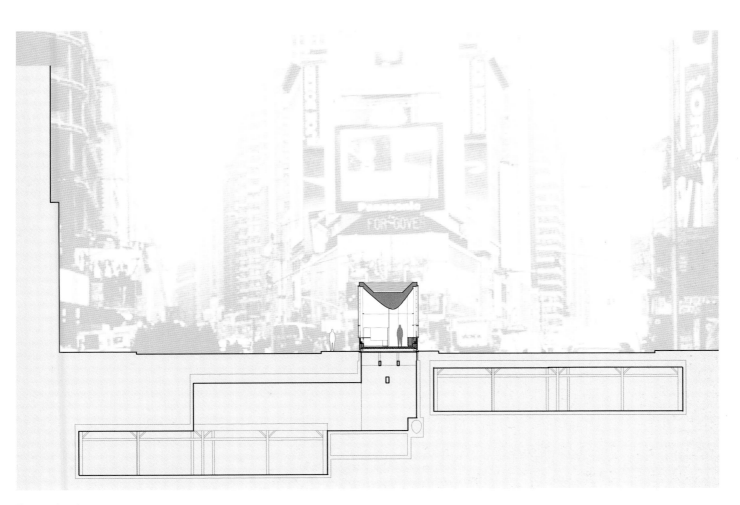

Transversal section

Detail of the main facade

Reason

I write for the purpose of nominating Steven Cassell and Adam Yarinsky of Architecture Research Office, specifically for US Armed Forces Recruiting Station, Times Square, New York, completed September 1999. As the name of the firm suggests, ARO is devoted to a research based architecture. The firm maintains a busy commercial practice, but utilizes these individual projects as a premise for research into materials and procedures of construction, the influence of codes and conventions, and the role of images and media. Hence innovation in their work emerges out of a process of inquiry.

The Times Square Recruiting Station is significant in that these young architects have been able to contribute a viable and interesting new piece of architecture to the public space of New York City. While this may be more common in Europe, it is quite exceptional here in the US. Moreover, the nature of the site and program are quite unique. On the one hand the architects have had to deal with the iconic condition of Times Square itself, and all of its associations. On the other hand, there is a strange mix of populism, advertising and politics that is associated with this particular program. The architects have responded by using an ephemeral media-based imagery for the building, turning the building itself into a kind of inhabited sign, but not in the Venturi sense. Rather than a decorated shed, the building is a partially transparent volume, where the signs are integrated into the spatial experience of the building. The appearance of the building changes from day to night, and from season to season, contributing a vital presence to the local streetscape.

It is a building that is at once an homage to the Times Square tradition of neon signs, and at the same time an innovative piece of architecture that suggest new possibilities for the use of graphics and media in architecture today. Although modest, it is an important new public building in New York, and a significant accomplishment for these young architects.
Stan Allen

CamenzindGrafensteiner AG

Stefan Camenzind
(Switzerland, 1963)
Michael Grafensteiner
(Switzerland, 1964)

Tyre-Fitting Shop/Art Exchange

Dimensions: 252 sq.m
Client: IWAG Distribution
Place of construction: Zurich, Switzerland
Date of completion: 2000

Office statement: process, teamwork and communication are the most important elements of our work. The process begins with us freeing ourselves from preconceived ideas by engaging in a wide collaboration with the client – the learning and understanding of clients' needs and requirements is a fundamental part of our design process.
Technology: we view technology as a means of enabling new ideas and concepts to achieve formulated objectives. It allows us to incorporate new, exciting environmental and economical concepts into our projects.
Local mapping: our work experience has taught us the importance of local events and microstructures. Especially important to our work, is the respect for people's local identity and roots. Identity is an energy neither visible nor stationary, but still essential to our daily well-being and, therefore, one of our fundamental criteria for spatial quality. By fusing the essential requirements of human identity with the project objectives, we aim to evolve projects with high architectural qualities. This, we see as the essence of our work as architects.

Architectural Competitions
First prize, sports centre Buchholz, Uster
First prize, communications centre siemens, Zurich
First prize, 12 apartments, Zurich
First prize, sports centre Hasenacker, Mannedorf
First prize, service centre Ara, Uster

Lectures
Building with steel 99, Luzern, Switzerland
Ravensbourne College of design and communication, Great Britain
Hochschule technik+architektur, Luzern, Switzerland
North Lancaster society of architects, Preston, Great Britain
Royal Institute of British Architects, London, Great Britain
University of Munich, Germany
University of Innsbruck, Austria
Prix fédéreaux des beaux-arts 1998, Schaffhausen, Switzerland

Completed work
Tyre-Fitting shop/Art exchange, Zürich, 2000
Sports Centre Buchholz, Uster , 1999

The new Tyre-Fitting shop/Art exchange is situated on a brownfield site adjacent to the lake of Zurich, between the railway station of Zurich-Wollishofen, a bus stop and the main access road into the centre of Zürich. The client was looking for a highly efficient tyre-fitting workshop with a strong visual identity.
Concept: The location of the site and its use as a tyre fitting workshop is typical of many cities that are encircled by a semi-industrial periphery serving the workforce commuting between their urban place of work and the surrounding suburban residential green belt. The semi-industrial fringe acts as a filter between an increasingly disassociated world of work and leisure that has developed into a finely tuned mirror of today's socio-economic changes. In this stark environment we find petrol stations, 24-hour shops, night clubs, factory outlets and start-up companies of every kind which are served by a never ending stream of people moving in and out of town. Movement is the key which drives this ever changing environment. We therefore conceived the entire facade of the first floor of this tyre-fitting building as a 4-sided, 200 m2 interactive communication surface. Sponsored by tyre manufacturers, young artists are given the opportunity to challenge the borders of art by taking their work out of the gallery and placing it into a commercial, fast moving environment. Challenging the conventional frontiers of art and commerce, the building becomes a marker of the cultural identity of today. The building acts as a drive-by gallery for passing vehicles and trains and engages even more powerfully with pedestrians waiting for buses or trains. This is the first building of a series of cultural markers we intend to place around the city of Zurich, acting as the new cultural gateway to the city. In the future, urban areas would be recognized by their cultural markers, rather than their historical heritage alone. Building The building footprint was established by optimising the very tight site constraints and the functional requirements of vehicle turning circles and working equipment. The building is split into two levels, with the workshop on the ground floor and tyre storage on the first floor.
Construction: Speed of construction and an early opening was essential to the client's business plan. Therefore the building was constructed as a steel frame with concrete floors and insulated metal tray panels, covered with a layer of glass as rain screen cladding. On the first floor, the metal panels were set back from the glass facade to create a 50cm wide access space, in which to install artwork. The architects were also responsible for the quantity surveying, as well as site management. This guaranteed a highly successful and fast transition from the first concept to the final construction in just 5 months.

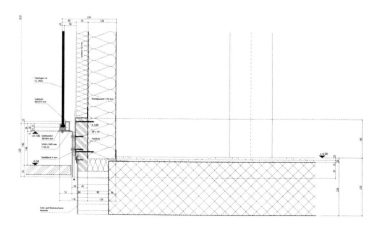

General view

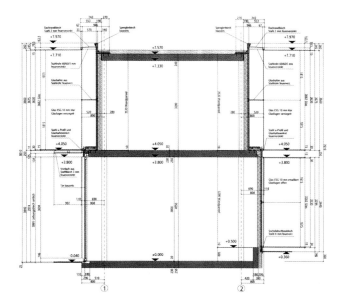

Detail on the tyre
fitting workshop at the
ground floor

Transversal section

Section: detail of the glass
facade

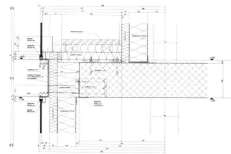

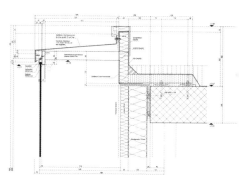

General view

General views

Reason

The Tire Shop/Art Gallery by Camenzind and Gräfensteiner in Zurich explores with particular clarity and effectiveness the theme of communication in the search for new forms of experimentation in defining contemporary urban space. The Swiss group understands that architecture has an extraordinary capacity to communicate. In this project, they investigate the communicative potential of architecture through the use of the most recent technological developments.
Marco Brizzi

Stefan Camenzind and Michael Gräfensteiner (C&G), winners of the British Young Architect of the Year 1999, were first widely recognized in 1998 for their Sport Center Buchholz in Uster Switzerland. Being trained as building technicians, they have a profound understanding of engineering. This, coupled with a wonderful ability to find simple but inspired solutions, is further complemented by a refined aesthetic sensibility.
In 2000, C&G built the Tire-fitting shop / art exchange in Zurich. The client was looking for a highly efficient tire-fitting workshop with a strong visual identity. The building is split into two levels, with the workshop on the ground floor and tire storage above.
It is situated on a brownfield site adjacent to the lake of Zurich, between a railway station, a bus stop and the main access road to town. The entire facade of the first floor was transformed into a 4-sided, 200 sq.m interactive communication surface where young artists are given the opportunity to place their work in the context of that uniquely fast-moving environment. Challenging the conventional frontiers of art and commerce, the building becomes a statement on the cultural identity of today, serving as a drive-by gallery.
Speed of construction was essential to the client's business plan. Therefore the building was constructed as a steel frame with concrete floors and insulated metal tray panels, covered with a layer of glass as rain-screen cladding. On the first floor, the metal panels were set back from the glass facade to create a 50cm wide access space in which to install the artworks.
The architects were responsible for quantity surveying, as well as site management which guaranteed a highly successful and fast transition from the original concept to the final construction, being realized in just 5 months. This 9 x 28 m building, with a volume of 1,975 cu.m, cost CHF 0.9 Mio ($ 0.5 Mio).
Jacqueline Burckhardt

The context of this urban object (should we call it architectural "Gimmick"?) is very seductive – on the one hand appearing something strange that is halfway between commercial activity (though not the kind that leads to poetic fantasy) and promotion for contemporary art, while on the other a challenge of urban chaos, which must be confronted from every possible angle.
The floor surface of the commercial activity is represented by a symbolic surface – the vertical and exhibitionist visibility of this urban cyma, which is the propelling element of art and culture in contemporary and urban keys for important signals such as publicity billboards or Daniere Shinjuku-style huge electronic screens.
The surrounding chaos is answered by focusing on a luminous object (night never falls, 24 hours a day…), the clearness and limpidness of which eclipse the surrounding disorder, keeping it at a distance.
The procedure is clear, precise and radical in its own way, the result therefore can appear seductive – as it was originally. But is this enough? Between the fleeting sentiment of " dèja vu " and the impression of architectural Calvinism as revenged aesthetic posture, a feeling of dissatisfaction remains. In a panorama of projects that are less convincing than you would be right to expect, this particular one stands out, you might say "frees itself", like a sportsman who wins by default, thereby denying us the real show and a kind of emotion.
Yves Nacher

Without reason.
Richard Burdett

Jae Cha
(India, 1970)

1992, graduated from Wellesley College, Bachelor in Arts in Architecture.
1993-1995, received Rotary Foundation Japan Scholar Fellowship to Tokyo.
1999, graduated from Yale University School of Architecture, Master in Architecture.
2000, established studio in Washington, DC.
Overall Prize winner, AR+D Emerging Architecture Award, *Architectural Review*, for Church in Urubo, Bolivia.
2001, adjunct professor at Renseleer Polytechnic Institute (RPI) in Troy, New York.

Church in Urubo, Bolivia

Dimensions: 113 sq.m
Client: Kie Dong Lee, Deuk 400 Jung
Place of construction: Urubo, Bolivia
Date of completion: 2000

This project is located in Urubo, a village near Santa Cruz, Bolivia. A small church of 113 square meters in area, it is made with local wood and translucent polycarbonate sheets. Donations for the project came from Bolivia and the United States. Planning took 8 months; the church was built in10 days by congregation members, local skilled workers, and volunteers from the United States.

Completed on August 4, 2000, the first service was held on August 6th. Well-planned and well-designed public spaces that meet the needs of a community are often overlooked as potential means to fighting poverty. Charitable contributions may reduce need, but ending poverty requires developing sustainable methods and encouraging a web of community interaction. Planned appropriately, a church can also function as day-care centre, vaccination centre, or public market. Flexible public spaces can provide the physical foundation for economically diverse, self-supported, and self-guided communities. We emphasize independence, rather than dependence, by seeking to create public spaces that offer direct paths to community empowerment and vitality.

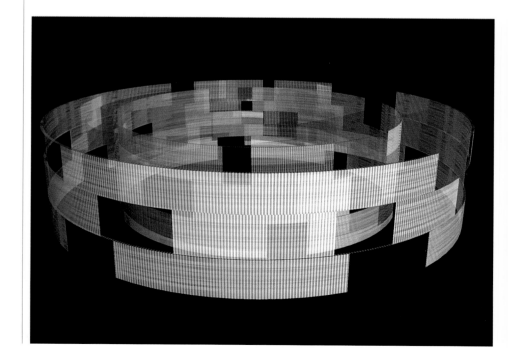

General view

Interior details

Reasons

For the "quality of space".
For the "intense feeling
of luminosity", achieved
with 'the simplest of
materials' and means.
For 'an exemplary
relationship between
architect and community',
a relationship and work
which has given birth
to a beautiful little piece
of architecture.
Quotes are from the
presentation of the
project as one of the
overall winners of the
AR+D awards in the
Architectural Review, Dec
2000. I found the jury
comments appropriate
and convincing, and
I am charmed and very
impressed by the project.
Klas Tham

The church in Urubo
seems to be of a striking
simplicity: a sort of a
primitive hut, a shelter for
meetings, but still with
a certain monumentality:
the walls remember the
textile walls Gottfried
Semper speaks about
to be at the origin of
monumental architecture.
It is the evidence that
there is no question about
ethics *or* aesthetics!
Martin Tschanz

Peter Ebner
(Austria, 1968)

Students Housing

Dimensions: 720 sq.m
Place of construction: Salzburg, Austria
Client: Austrian Student Foundation
Date of completion: 1999

Completed an apprenticeship as a carpenter.
Completed the school for mechanical engineering in
Salzburg.
Studied architecture at Graz (Austria) and UCLA (USA).
Until1995 Worked at Mark Mack Architects, Los
Angeles.
1995 Established Peter Ebner – Architecture, in
Salzburg.
1996–1998 member of the committee for Initiative
Architektur Salzburg.
Since 1998 established a Studio in Vienna.
Since 1998 collaboration with Franziska Ullmann.
Since 1998 president of the INITIATIVE ARCHITEKTUR
Salzburg.

Project-specific partnership with
Francis Soler, Paris.
atelier one, London.
Franziska Ullmann, Vienna.

Exhibitions
1999, Piranesi exhibition, Piran.
1999, 1070 Vienna, Vienna.
1999+2000, new Austrian architecture 1994-1999,
travelling exhibition.
2000, 8 visionary projects for Salzburg.
2000, emerging architects-Austria, travelling exhibition.

The city centre of Salzburg is shaped by the surrounding topography. The area with its rich history was settled in an arena between three characteristic ridges and a river, the Salzach, which further divided the area into sections. Sheer cliff walls constitute the backdrop for many buildings in the old inner city. The walls of the mountains and those of the buildings interact with each other, thus creating a main theme for the typical architecture of Salzburg.

The student hostel, which is used as a hotel during the summer season, incorporates business premises and a farmer's market on the ground level. The financial revenues of the hotel help to reduce the boarding cost for the students. The diverse needs of the occupants had to be respected, so that the lifestyle of the young scholars is not affected by the simplistic style of a hotel, and this is what gave this project such a wide spread definition.

The farmers market offers agricultural products directly from the producers. Each of the building's three usages is clearly defined in the project by a unique design. The transparent ground floor, above which the living quarters are located, is made up of crystalline structures containing the business premises, thus catching the visitor's eye.

They appear as boulders, which have fallen off the mountain, now resting below the softly curved building unit with its cellular living quarters. The curvature of the building not only allows

for two differently sized, dynamic squares, but at the same time it follows the natural curve of the Kapuzinermountain.

The facade, facing north towards the square, mirrors the parallel sequence of the hotel/student rooms in a discrete glass facade, which guarantees sufficient light in the mountain's cast shadow. The entrance divides the building in to two sections of different size. The front door presents itself as a tunnel, which opens up to a spacious hall, offering a wide view of the mountain.

The numerous references to the mountain, in a metaphorical sense, as well as the visual design create a new reference point in the topography of the old part of the city of Salzburg.

After finishing the Student housing it was not possible to get new work in Salzburg. The only work I received after finishing it, was to build the ground floor shops under the building.

Materials, construction: The student hostel is constructed with prefabricated concrete and surrounded by a glass facade, which is divided into three zones: the balustrade is panelled with translucent glass, the windows are transparent, and the lintel area is again in translucent insulated glass.

The business premise will be partially built this year, with glass and lightweight panel construction. The panelling is to be of either Niroster-steel or Corten-steel.

Relationship between
the new building and
the Kapuziner mountain

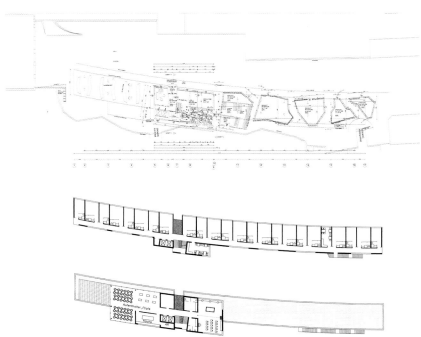

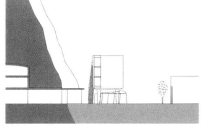

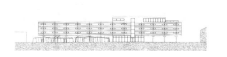

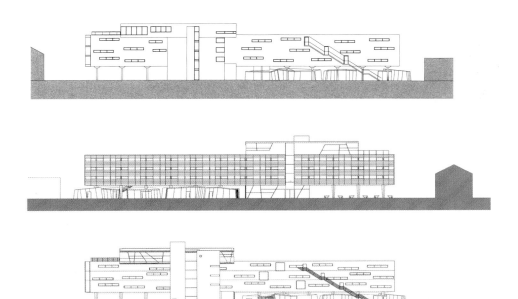

The main street facade

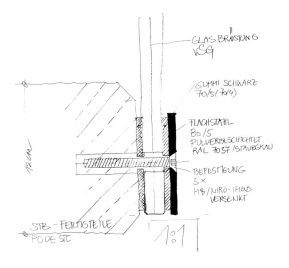

GLAS BRÜSTUNG
VSG

GUMMI SCHWARZ
70/5 (70/4)

FLACHSTAHL
80/5
PULVERBESCHICHTET
RAL 7037 /STAUBGRAU

BEFESTIGUNG
3 x
M8 /NIRO-IMBUS
VERSENKT

STB - FERTIGTEILE
PODESTE

12 cm

1:1

BV GLOCKENGASSE
DETAIL GLASBRÜSTUNG /BEFESTIGUNG / STIEGENHAUS
PODESTE

Detail of the main facade

The fire stairs

Interior details

Reason

The architecture of Peter Ebner shows a clear attempt to recognise the context and to respond to the provocation of a determined situation, but it is also an attempt to avoid the historic vocabulary, material or matrix.
The student's hostel which is used as a hotel during the summer season, incorporates business premises and a farmer market on the ground level. The financial revenues of the hotel help to reduce the boarding cost for the students. The diverse needs of the occupants had to be respected, so that the lifestyle of the young scholars is not effected by the simplistic style of a hotel, and this is what gave this project such a wide spread definition.
The farmers market offers agricultural products directly from the producers. Each of the building's three usages is clearly defined in the project by a unique design. The transparent ground floor, above which the living quarters are located, is made up of crystalline structures containing the business premises, thus catching the visitor's eye. They appear as boulders, which have fallen off the mountain, now resting below the softly curved building unit with its cellular living quarters. The curvature of the building not only allows for two differently sized, dynamic squares, but at the same time it follows the natural curve of the Kapuzinermountain.
The facade, facing north towards the square, mirrors the parallel sequence of the hotel/student-rooms in a discrete glass facade, which guarantees sufficient light in the mountain's cast shadow. The entrance divides the building into two sections of different size. The front door portrays a tunnel, which opens up to a spacious hall, offering a wide view of the mountain.
The numerous references to the mountain, in a metaphorical sense, the form of the building, as well as the visual design create a new reference point in the topography of the old part of the city of Salzburg.
Miha Desman

Shuhei Endo
(Japan, 1960)

Works
1994, Cyclestation M
1996, Healtecture K
1997, Transtation O
1998, Springtecture H
1999, Rooftecture Y; Rooftecture H
2000, Rooftecture K; Rooftecture B; Springtecture O.

Awards
1993, International Prize of architecture Andrea
Palladio, Italy.
1998, Asia Architecture Design Award, USA.
1999, Marble Architectural Awards 1998 East Asia
Grand Prix, Italy.
2000, 7th International Architecture Exhibition
Competitions of Ideas Città: Third Millennium Award,
Italy; ar+d Grand Award 2000 (The Architectural
Review)

Springtecture H

Dimensions: 119 sq.m
Client: Hyogo Prefecture
Place of construction: SHINgu-Cho, Hyogo, Japan
Date of completion: 1998

This is a facility in a small park sited in a highly artificial location which can be reached in one hour from Osaka, using the bullet train in the mountains of Hyogo Prefecture, Japan. As a facility for general use, of a kind that can be found anywhere in Japan, it defies expression of any regional character. Located in a park sandwiched by newly built elementary and secondary school buildings, the facility has a simple structure comprising three sections: a janitor's room, a men's room and a women's room. Public lavatories are required to provide convenience, based on openness, and security, deriving from closedness. This small facility, apparently a simple assemblage of parts, is described as "Halftecture" (half+architecture), since it is characterized simultaneously by both openness and closedness.

Openness is essentially the possibility of passage. In the case of this facility, however, passage is provided in three directions, with no clearly defined entrance. This avoids the defensiveness that is created, paradoxically, by demarcated openings and the transparency of glass; in other words making the whole facility a structure for passage, suggesting the possibility of entrance from almost anywhere. On the other hand, closedness as a spatial attribute is created by the use of corrugated steel sheet roofs, walls and floors, to which permeability is added by the 3.2 millimetre clearance of reversed steel sheets. The structure is basically in the form of an independent spiral of steel sheets, with gate shaped auxiliary materials partially inserted.

The architectural concept of this facility aims to form a linkage between openness and closedness through continuity of corrugated steel sheets. Interior walls double as exterior ceilings and floors, which also extend as exterior walls and roofs and once again turn into interior parts. The interior and exterior form a linkage of changes, challenging architectural norms expected by the observer, and suggesting a new, heterogeneous architectural form. The facility is also a small attempt towards a new architecture realized by continuous interplay between the interior and the exterior and the interactive effect of partial sharing of roofs, floors and walls.

Reasons

A simple industrial
element and a simple
natural movement
succeed in creating
an impressive and
congruous space with
its surroundings, in spite
of the industrial effect
of the materials.
Akram El Magdoub

Without reason.
Richard Burdett

Jakob + MacFarlane

Dominique Jakob
(France, 1966)
Brendan MacFarlane
(U.K., 1961)

Georges Restaurant,
Centre Georges Pompidou

Dimensions: 900 sq.m
Client: SNC Costes au Centre Georges Pompidou
Place of Construction: Paris, France
Date of completion: 2000

Dominique Jakob studied the history of art at the University of Paris I, and graduated from l'Ecole d'Architecture Paris-Villemin in 1991. He taught at l'Ecole Speciale d'Architecture from 1998 to 1999 and l'Ecole d'Architecture Paris-Villemin from 1994 to the present.
Brendan MacFarlane graduated from Southern California Institute of Architecture (SCI-Arc) in 1984. Taught at the same university and was an assistant at Harvard University from 1987 to 1989. In 1990, received the Master of Architecture, Graduate School of Design, Harvard University. Taught at the Bartlett School of Architecture from 1996 to 1998 in London and was a visiting teacher at l'Ecole Speciale d'Architecture from 1998 to 1999. Their principal projects are Maison T in Paris suburbs, the monument for Memory and Peace in Normandy and more recently the restaurant Georges on the sixth floor of Centre Pompidou .

The program brief was to create a restaurant on the sixth floor of the Centre Georges Pompidou. A space that would need to contain all the usual programmatic requirements of a restaurant, opening out onto an exterior terrace. The problem here was to create an appropriate response inside such a particular architectural context. Through working with the space, we became interested in the notion of trying to create an architecture that was made in a way, from what existed. Not wanting to import or create by addition, but propose the lightest possible intervention. Our interest was to discover or insert a kind of non-existent or background presence, maybe at the extreme, an almost non-architectural or non-designed response.

This is what lead us to become interested in working with the floor, proposing this surface as a new field of intervention, deforming it in such a way that we could insert a series of volumes beneath, thus creating a new landscape of both interior and exterior conditions, a hidden, maybe camouflage sit-

uation. This floor surface or "skin" we proposed to make out of aluminium, a material which when brushed both absorbs and reflects light, thus also reinforcing this notion of background; appearance and disappearance. A minimal presence, with a strong personality – using a kind of mask.

These series of volumes are slid beneath this skin: kitchen, bar, coat check and private reception room, finding their eventual form and position through the usual negotiation process of design. This skin acted also, as a stretchable surface that eventually absorbed all the programmatic changes. The project then became finalised at some point, caught or frozen in a state of movement. This sense was something we wanted to capture, creating an architecture that records the dynamic of program and actuality. Another aspect of our response to this site and specifically the floor as developable form, was in appropriating the building grid of Pompidou.

Every structural and surface increment is divisible into an 80 x 80 grid at the smallest, up to the primary structure of 12.80. This "real" grid, we appropriated as our "conceptual" one, which then becomes deformed by the volumes or pockets. Another way in which we confronted the site, was to work with the principle that all fluids arrive via the ceiling of the museum and then descend into each pocket, Pompidou as host, with each of the four pockets having their own system of air, water, electricity, a life support system of sorts.

Again this becomes part of a larger intention, to return the building system in order to dialogue with it, validating or referencing in doing so, part of a series of earlier ideas inherent in the architecture of the Centre, for example changeability, flexible systems, spontaneous systems, performance, etc. We designed the furniture in such a way that all pieces are aligned at 70 cm above the floor, in order to create a datum of furniture, making the outside terrace join seamlessly with inside space.

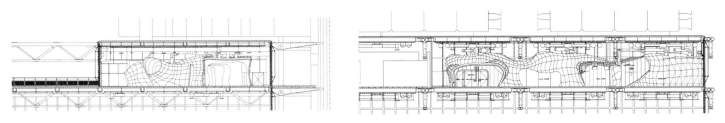

Main sections

Interior detail

Main view

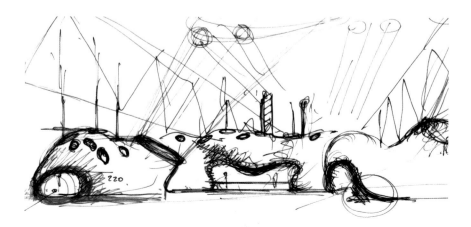

Details

Sketches and virtual
simulation

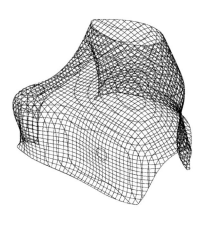

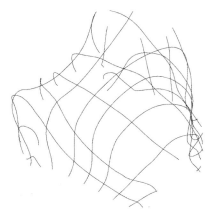

View from the terrace

Detail of an internal room

Restaurant's details

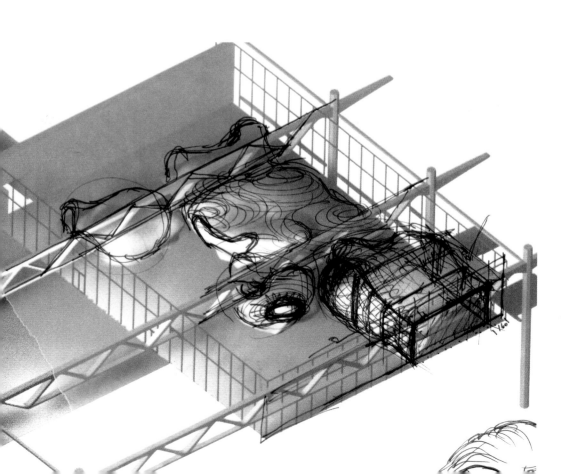

General sketch

General view from the
terrace

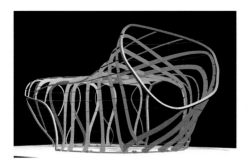

Digital simulation
and process making
of the internal room

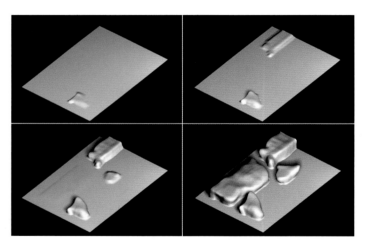
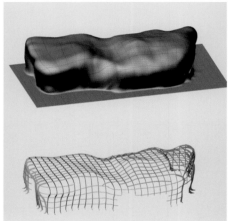

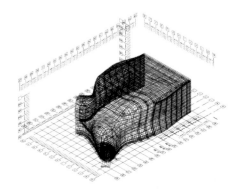
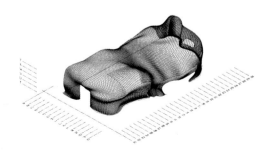

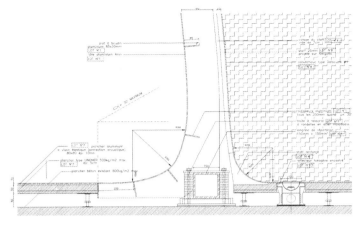

Detail

Reasons

The architects have been brave enough to face up to one of the most famous monuments of contemporary architecture without trying to obliterate it, but instead have a framed it using their own architectural language to conduct a dialogue between the 1970 and the present.
Deyan Sudjic

The architects have created an exceptional relationship between the containing space and the contents, in the development of a geometric-organic dialogue.
The project may be broken into geometric and organic spaces. The space in which the restaurant is located, the Centre Georges Pompidou, may be seen as the original geometric space which contains the restaurant as an organic entity in its interior space. The restaurant utilises interior elements which are geometric in contrast with the organic movement of people through the space. The play between geometric and organic spaces create a profound atmospheric rhythm.
Akram El Magdoub

Jacob+MacFarlane realized the Restaurant Georges on the fifth flour of the Centre Georges Pompidou in Paris. It is a surprising project in that its fluid configuration of space reinterprets, in a highly personal way, the idea of fluidity and transformability that characterizes the original structure of the building. The vivacity and sensitivity with which the new restaurant design reinterprets the dynamic quality found in the original structural plan by Piano and Rogers is parallel to the slightly ironic sense that characterizes this unique project.
Marco Brizzi

This conversion or infill of the Centre Georges Pompidou is almost a completion of the original design intentions 20 years later. The original building was realized in an impressive, expressive high-tech, but without the more playful aspects. Here it is almost as if some aspects of Archigram were added to that seriousness. The existent grid is brought to life. But at the same time it is a highly convincing, contemporary approach, using all the new possibilities computers offer in developing a scheme with a more fluid repertoire of forms, just as well as in executing these new fluid forms. The atmosphere in the restaurant is both serene and adventurous, not only offering a splendid view over Paris (as it always did) but also dividing the space in an almost nonchalant, relaxed way, without hiding or destroying the original idea of the building as a megastructure.
Bart Lootsma

71

Jean-Philippe Lanoire
(France, 1965)
Sophie Courrian
(France, 1963)

Renovation of Shed 14
in Bordeaux

Dimensions: 6754 sq.m
Client: Comune di Bordeaux
Place of construction: Bordeaux, France
Date of completion: 1999

They obtained their diploma in from the School of Architecture of Bordeaux in 1993.

Diploma projects
A communication and exhibition space for architecture, hangar 11.
A sunset observatory in Alcatraz.
Participation in the Arc En Rêve Exhibition in 1994:
7 studies-completion works at the School of Architecture of Bordeaux.
Winners of the "Butagaz" competition.
Their office was established at the end of 1996.

Philosophy
- Y belief.
- Being free electrons, free to be independent or to be related or complementary to someone else.
- Working only with people with whom there is some kind of feeling.
- Zapping: from public work orders to international competitions, from the restoration of the H14 in Bordeaux to an exhibition area for fluctuating architecture in Almere, from the drawing of the mobile material for the tram company in Bordeaux to a maritime station in Marseille... Moving.
- Make others like you.

The program: renovation of a shed to be used for a large exhibition hall.
The location: the river-front of the left side between the street that runs along the "facade" of the river-front and the Garonne.
The renovation of Shed 14 represents the first step towards re-conquering these four kilometres of unused public space of harbour area in a zone of public space and the reclaiming of the river as part of the city.
The sheds: they have been imagined and built as valid and effective devices, constructed in series according to a longitudinal logic based on the direction of the maritime traffic; they are part of Bordeaux's sentimental and historical heritage. Shed 14 is a two floor building made out of concrete with a 6m/6m structure.
The project: our intention was to respect the existing shed's structure and image, conferring it the status of a public building, having it participate in a global wish to open the city towards the river. The ground floor preserves the concrete structure of the existing building. The columns were eliminated on the upper level thus creating an exhibition platform completely free from any influence or pre-existing elements; the roof was also raised. We therefore have the shed's renovated antique part relative to the side that faces the city and its two embankments. The pattern and the mouldings were maintained. The concrete was restored and painted, the metal lathing grids were placed in the openings existing in the facade. The building's coarse and industrial aspect was preserved. On the river side, the building is completely open towards the river along the river-front walkway. The front of this facade is animated by eight emergency stairways in galvanized steel which present shiny oblique lines. This listel facade diffuses an opalescent light. Movement is given to the front of this facade with the use of eight emergency stairways in galvanized steel having shiny oblique lines. They are placed within a large deck in Ipé extending the floor's interior space. This deck, a sort of balcony, offers a privileged view overlooking the Garonne and the city. The facade of the floor that overlooks the deck is based on an alternating, but precise, rhythm of six meters of transparent glass windows and translucent listel windows.

This facade therefore is made entirely of glass and opens out on the river bank, a sort of window. At night, from the other bank of the river it appears as a luminescent bar overlooking the river fronts.

This facade extends and projects through the volume formed by the entrance. This type of box constitutes on one hand the symbol of the entrance into the building while also the building's identifying sign and mark in the city. Glazed to a height of 2.1 metres, it is clad with double layer polycarbonate for its remaining height. The part in glass is covered on the exterior by a netted lathing in galvanized steel. Vertical neon lights, installed in a "quinconcial" way on the interior create a constellation of light in this translucent volume that becomes the luminescent signal of the building's activity in the city. In carrying out this project, our intention was to discretely restore the parts that were maintained, fully respecting their identity. We wanted to respect the building's logic and history, using new elements in series and using raw materials. We wanted to express the building's modernity through the use of these new elements.

Our wish was to open the building towards the river and have it participate through its architecture in the future walk along the river fronts and their re-evaluation.

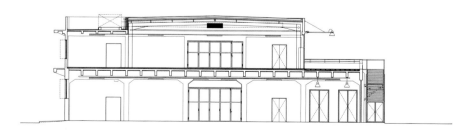

General view and detail
of the external stairs

Ground floor and first floor

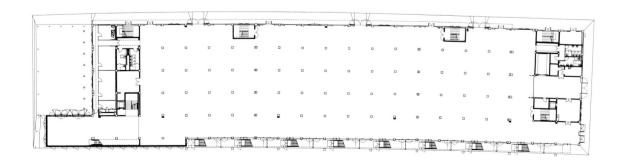

The stairs and the terrace

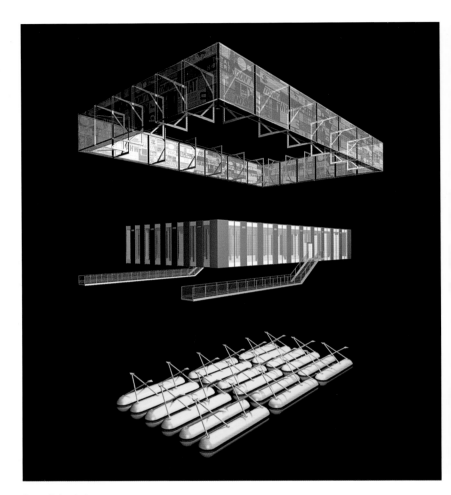

General simulation

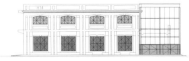

External fronts

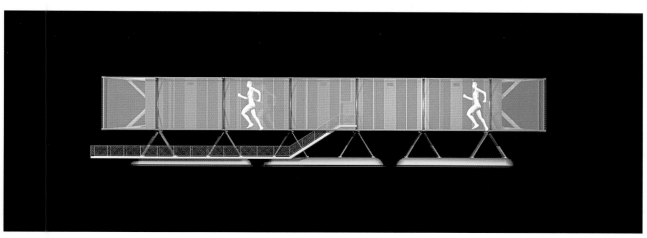

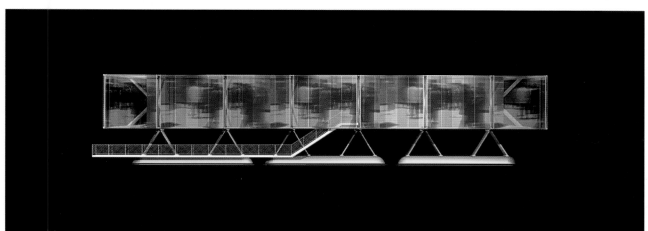

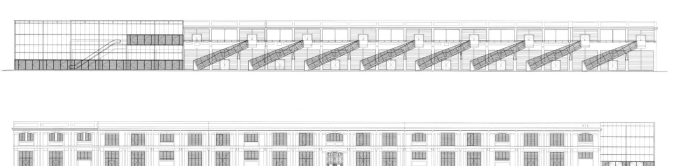

Interior's details

Night views of the main
entrance

The main front on the
river

Reasons

This project is a prime
example of the concerns
that have been addressed
in recent architectural
projects in France. It is a
project which forefronts
the materials and
processes of recycling. It
is a project that begins by
examining the economy
of recycled materials
and resources and then
recognises the opportunity
to create new form and
function in obsolete or
abandoned buildings.
The images of this project
succinctly reflect a deep
understanding of new
technological systems.
Camilo Salazar

A brilliant transformation
of an existing building
where the various old and
new industrial elements
blend and overlap.
Mirko Zardini

Alfredo Paya Benedito
(Spain, 1961)

University Museum in Alicante

Dimensions: 15.262 sq.m
Client: Universitary Museum in Alicante
Place of construction: Alicante, Spain
Date of completion: 1998

Teaching Experience
1991-1999, 1999-2001, Design Professor at the Technical Superior School of Architecture of Valencia, Spain.
2000-2001, Design Professor at the Technical Superior School of Architecture of Alicante, Spain.
Guest Teacher In Several Universities and Habitual Lecturer In Different Institutions.

Major Competitions
1985, First Prize, National Competition Office Building for the Local Government of Alicante, Spain.
1988, Fist Prize, International Competition European I, Burriana, Castellon, Spain.
1988, Finalist, International Competition European I, Madrid, Spain.
1994, First Prize, National Competition University Museum, University of Alicante, Spain.
1995, First Prize, National Competition Center of Chemical Technology, University of Alicante, Spain.
2000, First Prize, Restricted Competition Youth House In Quart, Valencia, Spain.

Major Awards for Projects
1996, Prize, Architects Association Comunidad Valenciana, Health Center In Elche, Alicante, Spain.
1997, Prize, 4th Biennial of Spanish Architecture, Office Building for Local Government of Alicante.
1997, Honour Mention, Spanish Federation of Stone, Office Building for Local Government of Alicante, Spain.
1998, Prize, Young Spanish Architecture Antonio Camuñas Foundation.
1998, Prize, Architecti. Centro Cultural De Belem, Lisboa, Portugal, University Museum, Alicante.
1998, Selected, Ii Meeting Portuguese-Spanish of Architecture.
1998, Finalist, Vi Edition Mies Van Der Rohe Prize European Architecture, University Museum, Alicante.
1999, Finalist, Fad Prize, University Museum of Alicante, Spain.
1999, Finalist, 5th Biennial Spanish Architecture , University Museum of Alicante, Spain.
2000, Selected, Spanish Pavilion 7th International Biennale of Architecture, Venice, Italy.

On the edge of a campus, defined by the highway and the mountains in the distance, the mirroring image of a round box floating in a great dug-out space announces the building. It is apparently inaccessible. At the edge of the lake, the land dips. Like a mole, the visitor gradually discovers the deep excavation which marks the route around the various rooms.

The stone which surrounds the excavation seems always to have been there, as though we had found it there when we set to digging. In this way, the land/terrain becomes an enclosure where the different artistic activities will take place.

The patio – a void – is the element that articulates the different parts of the museum while also forming a lovely place for meditation and repose. Every part of the building can be reached from here: the rooms of the multi-purpose museum, the open-air auditorium, the covered hall and the box.

These four pieces on a single ground plan define two parallels that talk to each other two by two. On the one hand, the museums communicate through their circulation spaces, on the other, the auditoriums, face to face, can be integrated into each other – as the front of the covered hall´s stage can be folded away in order to join the two together.

The "box", the space that will house the permanent collection, the protagonist of the ensemble, has been thought like a very high block, weightless, with a small scratch at its lower end so that there is total permeability with the patio. The volume of the box and the treatment of the light will give certain impression of infinity. The cavity between its thick double walls houses the piping and wiring as well as the audio-visual elements such as projectors, screens, videos, etc., thus constituting an interactive space. A strict modulation connects all the ambits, generating an order which facilitated the construction. The only way out for this enclosure, isolated from the outside, is via views of far-off arid, mountainous landscape. The empty interiors are bathed in overhead light.

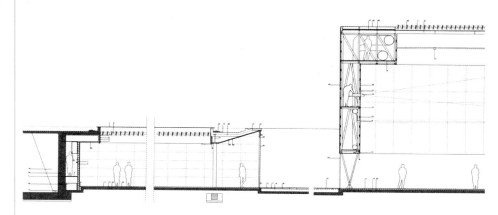

General view

Main entrance

The museum's patium

Details

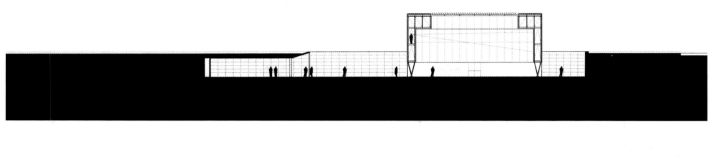

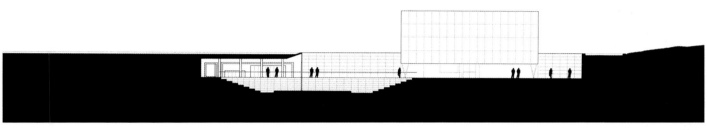

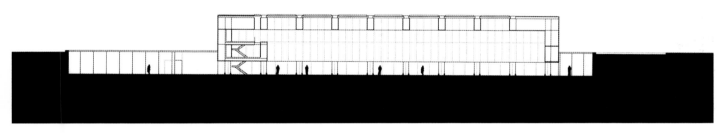

Longitudinal and
transversal section

Main floor

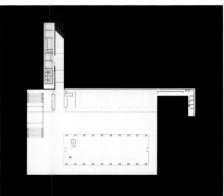

Reason

Pandora's box: the
architect has perforated
and excavated the rock,
obtaining a sort of stone
box open up to the sky.
Then, to house the
museum, he located a
wooden box, creating an
extremely fascinating
space.
The wooden box is
supported by a solid
metal structure painted
in white, which shows
an ingenious system of
joints. The result is a
fascinating modern space,
pervaded by a deeply
moving sense of eternity.
A real masterpiece.
Professor PAYÁ is a
fantastic Spanish young
architect. He was
my student in Madrid
and graduated with
a first-class thesis.
He then worked in
the Mediterranean, in
Alicante, where he lives
and teaches. He has
won many competitions,
and received many
acknowledgments. His
small but excellent work
is already widely known.
A finalist at the Mies Van
der Rohe Award, his work
was also exhibited at the
Biennial in Venice last
year. He's a wonderful
architect and a splendid
professor.
Alberto Campo-Baeza

The classified architects

5+1

Paola Arbocò (Italy, 1965)
Pierluigi Feltri (Italy, 1962)
Alfonso Femia (Italy, 1966)
Gianluca Peluffo (Italy, 1966)
Maurizio Vallino (Italy, 1967)

University Campus in the Old Barracks Bligny

Dimensions: 7000 sq.m
Client: Società di Promozione degli Enti Savonesi per l'Università
Place of construction: Savona, Italy
Date of completion: 1999

The 5+1 associati office was established in Genoa in 1995. Its architects graduated from the Faculty of Architecture of Genoa and presently collaborate on the architectural design courses of Prof. E. D. Bona at the University of Genoa. In 1995 they published the book *A Carnevale anche i grattacieli ballano. Ancora 106 frammenti sulla città di New York* (*Even skyscrapers dance for Carnival. Another 106 fragments on New York City*), published by JoshuaLibri. In 1996 they won the first prize at the national competition for signs designing for the Campi industrial park in Genoa. In 1996 they published the book *Francia 2013 - Italia 10. Non si uccide anche così l'architettura? Note, commenti e suggestioni a margine dei concorsi di architettura* (*France 2013 – Italy 10. Isn't this another way of killing architecture? Notes, comments, and perceptions around architecture competitions*), published by JoshuaLibri. In 1997 they edited a series on JA architecture for JoshuaLibri, in co-operation with Yves Nacher. In 1996 they won the competition for the new Hospital in Biella. They have been members of IFYA (International Forum Young Architects) since 1997. In the same year "S.p.e.s. spa" assigned them the working out of the project for the conversion of the former Bligny barracks in Savona into a new University Campus. In 1998 they were invited by the Italian Institute for Culture in Paris to display "il cammino delle idee" (the route of ideas) in an exhibition entitled: "5+1 associati: progetti in gruppo. Fin qui tutto bene" (5+1 associati: team group projects. So far, so good). The related catalogue was published by Joshua. In 1999 they won the tender for the new archaeological centre in Aquileia. In 1999 they took part in the Biennial of Young European and Mediterranean Artists - held in Rome (May / June) - displaying their work at the "Gerico" exhibition, and a self-portrait of their office in the "grande ét@gere". In 2000 INARCH invited them to exhibit their work at the Italian Institute for Culture in Prague and at the Biennial in Venice. Both exhibitions were dedicated to young Italian architects. Still in the year 2000 they won the competition for an office building in Vado Ligure, and were invited to the second stage of the international competition for the Congress Bridge in Rome. In the first months of 2001 their works are on display as part of a dedicated exhibition, "5+1 architetti associati, Genova. L'ombra delle idee" ("5+1 architetti associati, Genoa. The Shadow of Ideas") at the ETH, Eidgenössische Technische Hochschule, GTA Institut für Geschichte und Theorie der Architektur of Zurich. On that occasion a monograph will be published by Skira, edited by Sebastiano Brandolini.

The project is intended to satisfy the functional requirements of a university campus, within a facility like the former Bligny barracks, which had been designed for uses radically different from those of university education and training.

From the architectural standpoint, the following requirements were therefore set as clear objectives: responding to innovative technical and functional requirements; radically transforming the image of the barracks complex; functionally linking the neighbourhood and the city.

The intervention's guiding spirit was, on the whole, that of eliminating the barriers separating the barracks from the city, thereby permitting perceptive and functional permeability, and stressing and enhancing its link through neighbourhood activities, sports, production, and training (stadium and pool, productive settlements, building school).

One of the first and most essential design choices was that of moving the entrance to the area, in order to create visual and functional linkage to the city. In fact, the area immediately adjacent to the entrance was designed as a more "urban" space within the campus, with two new buildings – the gym and the cafeteria – in functional contact with the city, and a piazza that may be used as an open-air theatre.

The green spaces and sports facilities were redesigned from the standpoint of an "urban campus," playing on the contradiction between respecting the study and work areas and the neighbourhood's and the city's need for sporting and cultural spaces and services. In parallel, the transformation of the existing buildings, which are hidden, opaque, and inward-looking at present, moves in the direction of opening, making transparent, and innovating the campus's image.

The main intervention on the C-plan former dormitory buildings was cutting the central part by demolishing the body connecting the two wings of the dormitories. This operation made it possible to: simplify distribution from the standpoint of circulation and safety; re-modulate the size of the existing buildings into sizes that are easily compatible with the needs expressed by the customer and the spaces' required flexibility; lighten the pressure of the long frontage on the avenue, freeing the transversal vision.

The system of canopies and wooden pavement virtually extend the buildings along the main avenue and make it possible to vary the perception

of the paths, which are no longer so banally straight.

The brise-soleil system, which produces an effective passive heat protection system on the roof, continues in part on the façades to screen the large openings provided for in the design. In fact, the prospects were redesigned, with the windows enlarged and vertical light cuts created – interventions necessary for a building that now functions mainly for the daytime, but that beforehand had been designed for the night-time and rest.

In the two buildings, the former kitchen and the former cafeteria, positioned in the upper part of the area, the programme's representation and communications functions are located. Due to its morphological and functional features, this portion of the design has been dubbed the "Acropolis."

Underneath the large concrete vault of the former cafeteria are housed the library and its facilities – environments that require filtered light and that at the same time need to relate with the exterior space. Therefore, the side openings and the entire lower perimeter architecture have been redesigned. A longitudinal garret exploits the height of the vault and makes it possible to house the media centre, the documentation centre, and the data bank in a position autonomous yet visually linked to the library.

The interior of the former kitchen building is to house the 350-seat auditorium, which completes the system's equipment, thereby bridging a gap in the area's function and image. The space around the building has also been designed to be available for the open-air work, exploiting the broad spans of shade from the canopies that reconstitute the formal unit of the two buildings.

The system of exterior spaces is marked by various pavements differentiating the various types of path, alternating portions made with self-locking elements and printed asphalt for vehicles and portions in vibrated cement, architectural concrete, stabilized earth, and wood for those moving about on foot. Each material corresponds with different tactile sensations and different speeds of movement: earth for standing, vibrated cement for rapid movements, and wood for crossing links.

The system for lighting the exterior spaces alternates portions with overhead lighting, floodlights placed under trees, and spotlights from above the canopies that bring the buildings into relief, leaving the paths slightly shaded. Crossing guides and floodlights at ground level complete the system.

General view

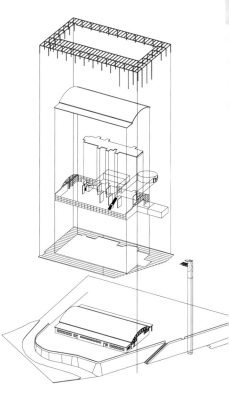

General plan and
axonometric scheme

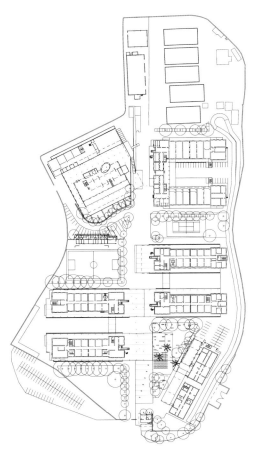

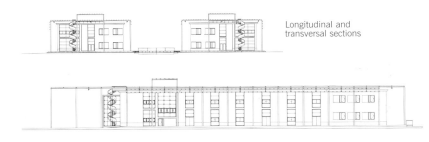

Longitudinal and
transversal sections

Reason

The realization of the
University Campus
of Savona and the
refurbishing of the former
Bligny barracks on the
part of 5+1 Associates
in collaboration with
Chaix Morel and
Associates, represents
a case worthy of attention
both for the high
quality reached in the
composition and
realization of the work,
and for the capability of
the designers to effectively
blend research conducted
locally in Genoa with
significant international
collaborative experiences.
This formula is among
the most interesting
elements at the basis
of the project's highly
deserved success.
Marco Brizzi

David Adjaye
(Tanzania, 1966)

Elektra House

Dimensions: 130 sq.m
Client: anonymous (two artists)
Place of construction: Whitechapel, London, UK
Date of completion: 2000

David Adjaye is the principal of Adjaye & Associates, a London-based architecture firm. He recently refurbished the new headquarters for CABE (Commission on Architecture and the Built Environment) and his firm has received a commission to design a retail floor in the new Selfridges department store in Birmingham. His client list includes homes for the artists, Chris Ofili and Jake Chapman, and for the actor, Ewan McGregor. In addition, his studio is working on two school projects, one in West Africa and the other in Massachusetts, United States.
He received his master in Architecture (1993) from the Royal College of Art where he currently teaches and he has lectured at the Harvard Graduate School of Design, Institute for Contemporary Art, Royal Society of Arts and Whitechapel Gallery.

The clients, an artist and a sculptor with two small children, own the one storey belt factory site. They desired a flexible home which would contain a live/work space, as well as three bedrooms. The site is situated in London's East End, an eclectic and industrial neighbourhood and they had a building budget of £ 80,000.

The initial concept was to make a house within a house. This comes out of a structural economy – making use of the existing boundary walls and foundations. A new steel frame is inserted inside the site boundary which makes the roof for the entire project and the sleeping spaces for the house. The facades are hung off the steel frame, allowing a small load to be transferred onto the existing footings.

The front of the house faces north and is conceived as an insulated facade with no aspect. The exterior of the house is clad in one material – a resin coated plywood, normally used for shuttering. The boards are arranged in a stereometric pattern, whose proportions rhyme with the windows of the neighbourhood. The material is left in its natural state – and resembles a purple-bronze finish. The house, which ends a typical East End terrace, is reflective and shimmers in contrast to the surrounding Victorian brickwork.

The mute elevation is expressed in the interior as a double height space with a continuous skylight running the length of the house. This space acts as a light chimney for the flexible live/work space on the ground. The back of the house faces south and enjoys the full east to west aspect. This is exploited by making a large glazed clerestory and reflecting wall, creating a second double height space, which scoops sunlight into the ground floor. Four by one metre double glazed units are glued into aluminium frames, running to the top of the parapet and are held by a steel I-section beam which runs the length of the house. Underneath these panels the elevation is divided in two; on the right side is a glazed box and on the left a concertina window system opens onto a walled court space. Raised 40 cm above the ground floor, this space is decked with stained exterior wood planks. The west elevation has one large tinted window which is shared by the two principal bedrooms.

One enters the house through a side passage at the rear. The ground floor is an continuous underfloor heated space, undulating between outdoor courtyard, flexible live/work room, dining room and kitchen. The floor of this space is an unsealed concrete screed. The upper floor is entered on the east side by a maple staircase. This material continues into all the rooms.

The upstairs is conceived as five formal rooms, a hallway which is accentuated by the halo skylight above all the doors, a suite of three bedrooms and a bathroom. The rooms are small but the floor to ceiling heights are deliberately tall (3.2 metres).

Each room has a full height door which is the same thickness as the wall construction. Each room has a skylight which is positioned to reflect as much light into the rooms. The skylights are inclined in a specific direction resulting in a clock-like effect. The traditional and functional idea of light from a window illuminating a room has been reversed. In the Elektra House, light is a phenomenological presence. Its properties of reflection, luminosity and movement are the experiences of the house.

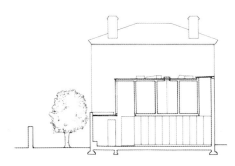

General view from the inner courtyard

Front street

Details of the interior

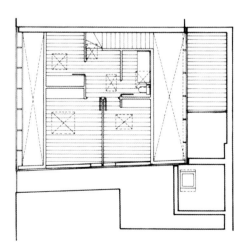

Ground and first floor

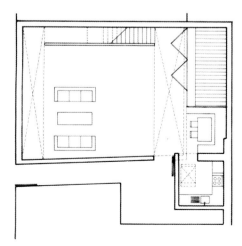

Reason

A first house, especially one achieved with a remarkably restricted budget – less than $ 1500, might not seem like the most appropriate way to judge the calibre of a young architect. But there is something compelling about Adjaye's house in London's East End built for a young family. It rejects the conventional wisdom of context, without being distruptive. Using the minimum of precious materials it creates a powerful sense of architecture as a modifier of light and space. The house is like a camera, presenting a series of cropped and edited outlooks; on the sky; on the crumbling brickwork of the next door house just two, metres away. It sits on the street like as well be lead or concrete. Inside the bedrooms and bathrooms hang in a tray suspended from the roof into the main living space, making it double height at front and back. Taken with the rest of Adjaye's growing workload, it suggests a rich architectural potential.
Deyan Sudjic

Jesús Mª Aparicio Guisado
(Spain, 1960)

Apartment Building

Dimensions: 2310 sq.m
Place of construction: Santa Marta De Tormes, Salamanca, Spain
Date of completion: 1998

Degree in Architecture at Escuela Técnica Superior de Arquitectura de Madrid (ETSAM), with Honors in both Building Design and Urban Design in 1984, where he tought Elements of Composition.
Prize of Rome in Architecture at the Academia de Bellas Artes de España in Rome and Fulbright/ M.E.C Fellowship. He was Visiting Scholar at Columbia University, New York, where he obtained a Master in Architecture and Building Design. Ph.D. in Architecture and since 1996 Tenured Professor of Building Design at the ETSAM. Has been Visiting Professor at the schools of Architecture of the Politecnico of Milano, Architectural Association of London, Darmstadt Institute of Technology, Paris-Belleville, Universitá Di Roma "La Sapienza", Universitá di Napoli and Harvard University. City pf Madrid Architecture and Urbanism Prize, A.P.D. Design Prize, HYSPALIT Prize of Brick Architecture and Special Mention in the European Architecture Award Luigi Cosenza 2.000. In June 2000 he represented Spain at the Bienale di Architettura di Venezia.

Concrete, brick and stone: A concrete base, a perforated, scratched and pierced brick box. Perforated in the bedrooms to force the exterior to penetrate, scratched in the living rooms to form continuity with the exterior, pierced in the attic by an interior that overflows so much walled-in containment.

The attic is the summit of the construction, it is an habitable plane between walls of brick and lime, a floor of stone and the blue of the sky. The rooms flee from the enclosure. An escape accentuated by concrete boxes that make the spatial intent of the interior compatible with the exterior reality.

Water basins underline the paradisiacal space of the summit. A built, unified, hermetic and stereotomic box. Concrete, brick and stone. Apartments of air and sky.

General view

Roof detail

Reasons

A house made of air and sky
Aparicio's houses in Salamanca are a first-rate work, mainly for the sense of strength they convey. A brick box includes a programme of council houses, crowned by a cement penthouse, open up to the sky and onto the surrounding landscape.
The houses layout is exact and orderly. The penthouse, so close to the sky, is glorious. The setback required by the law is used to create, together with the partition walls which surround it, beautiful open-air patios – Le Corbusier's "chambre au ciel ouvert".
Holes in the wall capture the outside landscape, marking it with large and clean-cut cement boxes. It is a house made of air and sky.
Professor Aparicio is one of the greatest Spanish young architects. He not only attended the Spanish Academy of S. Pietro in Montorio in Rome as a resident student; he also won a Fulbright, thanks to which he attended the Columbia University for 2 years. There, he worked on his Ph. D. thesis, which was then published in Argentina in a wonderful book in Spanish, *The Wall*.
His short but rich architectural production includes a fitting-out work for Terragni's exhibition in Madrid, and the council houses in Salamanca, a strong and wonderful work. Both works were granted an award.
He recently won a competition for a very interesting hotel in Salamanca, whose construction-works are going to start soon.
As far as his teaching career is concerned, he is a distinguished professor at the Madrid School.
Alberto Campo Baeza

ARCHEA

Marco Casamonti
(Italy, 1965)

Centro Divertimenti Stop Line

Dimensions: 2310 sq.m
Client: Golf Parco dei Colli S.p.A.
Place of construction: Curno, Bergamo, Italy
Date of completion: 1998

Graduated in 1990 in Florence, where he lives and is engaged in his professional practice with the Archea office, established in 1988.
In 1994 he became a full member of the Area editorial office, as an editorial consultant.
Since 1997 he has been the editor of the international architectural magazine "Area". He is also the editor of the architectural section of the Federico Motta Editore publishing house. He has also been the editor of the magazine "Materia" since 1999.
He has taken part in many national and international competitions, such as the International Competition for the Japan National Library, Kansai-kan of the National Diet Library (mentioned project) (1996).
In 1997 he took part, together with Prof. Loris Macci, in the competition for the construction of an office building for the firm ZIPA, based in Ancona, winning the second prize. With Prof. A. Cortesi he participated in the competition for a "new gate for the town" in Parma, winning, once again, the second prize.
In 1994 he won the first prize for the piazza Vittoria in Castiglioncello (Livorno).
In 1999 he came third in the competition for the building of the IUAV offices in Venice. The following year he ranked second in the competition for the New Base of the Italian Space Agency in Rome.
In 1995 he realised an Entertainment Centre, the "Stop Line Entertainment Centre". A monograph was then dedicated to this project, *The new global theatre*, published by Alinea.
In 1998 he took part in the National Competition for the "Trade and Business Centre" in Calenzano, in co-operation with Studio Archea, Ipostudio, and Elio di Franco. This project was the winner of the competition.
In 1999 he held a series of conferences (Architectural Routes) at the Faculty of Architecture of Genoa, and participated in the Conference on Design organised by the Brescia Municipality.
The new Municipal Library of Curno (Bergamo) and a large square in Merate – with an open-air theatre, an underground car park, and a small museum pavilion – are currently under construction.
Marco Casamonti is presently a member of the scientific committee of the exhibition on street furniture, organised in Lucca by Lucense.

Stop Line is probably the most unusual multimedia and multifunction center to be built over the last few years, comprising large spaces, sophisticated equipment, various attractions and huge parking spaces. The Center includes an ice-skating rink, disco, bars and restaurants, bowling alleys and billiard room, video games, and a wide range of other activities. not only fulfills young people's desire for a meeting place, but also the needs of many other people including music, entertainment and places to eat.

These premises can be transformed each evening and thereby continuously propose sophisticated and new attractions. There is nothing repetitive about Stop Line and time passes through a series of happenings and surprises.

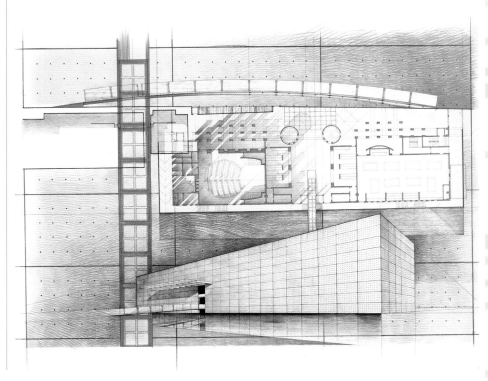

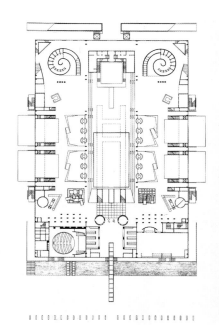

Ground floor

Details of the external facade

The entrance and the
main hall

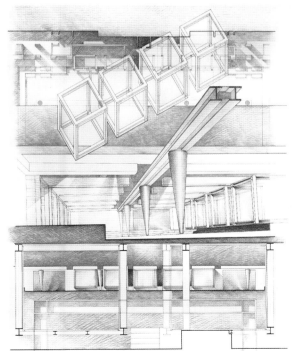

Sketches

Reason

This project is among
the most original centers
devoted to recreational
activities built in
Italy. Stop Line contains
a skating rink, a
discotheque, a restaurant-
bar, a bowling alley and
other game areas. A stage
is particularly suitable
for hosting events such
as concerts, conferences,
fashion-shows, etc. This
is an existing building
which is being reused.

Inside, the areas and
the space have been
arranged and recreated
playing creatively on the
juxtaposition between
the heaviness of the
metal, both colored and
natural, and the lightness
of glass. It is project
that demonstrates
how architecture can
play a spectacular and
recreational role that is
dynamically interactive
with those who use it.
Livio Sacchi

Architectural Office Casagrande & Rintala

Marco Casagrande
(Finland, 1969)
Sami Rintala
(Finland, 1971)

Architectural Office Casagrande & Rintala was established in 1998 by architects Marco Casagrande and Sami Rintala. Besides normal architectural work we design architectural installations, landscape installations, theatre and dance performances, video and multimedia works commenting on society and the environment, run workshops and give lectures.

Buildings
Uunisaari summer Helsinki, 2000.
Theatre Pekkaniska shelter Vantaa, 2000-2002.
Interiors misc.

Installations
Land(e)scape Architectural Review's AR+D Emerging Architecture Award, 1999.
Sixty Minute Man Venice Biennale, 2000.
Convoy 4th international conference of environmental aesthetics, 2000.
1000 Peace Flags realized winning entry, national landscape-art competition 2000, Quezalcoatlus Havanna Biennale.
2000, Yokohama Triennale.
2001, Firenze Biennale.

Sixty Minute Man

An archaic oak park was planted inside a 34 meters long freight barge, which was found unused in the Laguna of Venice. The park is growing on top of the equivalent of 60 minutes worth of composted human waste from the city of Venice. The ship was taken to the Arsenal harbour and opened as a public park, commenting on the Biennale theme "City, less aesthetics, more ethics."

The rusting freight barge "Topogigio" was found, filled with mud and dirt, at the port of Chioggia. The vessel was cleaned and the necessary openings were cut in order to create a series of spaces. The gangways from the quay up to the boat and down to the cargo space are made out of iron elements, used in Venice for reinforcing the islands.

The exact amount of biologically cleaned and composted human waste "produced in 60 minutes was then placed in the cargo hold of the barge. On top of the composted waste is a layer of white gravel, from which rises a small stand of oaks. A watering system for the park is installed into the soil.

The 22 oaks planted on the human waste symbolize the simple way of living and the eternal circulation of organic material. The leaf crowns are partly visible from the quay, but one can not see the park itself until you climb a gangway to the deck of the barge. From there, you descend another ramp into the trees.

Benches line the sides of the barge interior. An old crane of the Arsenal harbour looms above. Otherwise the walls block the cityscape, you can see only the sky above. Standing in the shadowy park one can sense the moving of the ground.

All the material is recycled – put together to create an architectonic collage. The oaks would have a full lifetime with the energy of the human waste produced by Venetians in one hour.

Architectonic installation at the 7th International Venice Biennale of Architecture 2000
Dimensions: 238 sq.m
Client: La Biennale di Venezia
Place of construction: Arsenale di Venezia
Date of completion: 2000

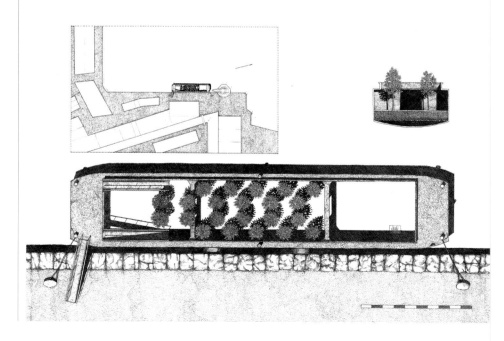

Patio's details

Reason

I enjoyed the re-assemblage of conditions specific to the city of Venice, and the intelligent use of opportunities offered to the architects. The construct perform well in its context. Also commendable are the designer's restraint, by which the assemblage has been effected.
Anand Bhatt

Atelier van Lieshout

Joep Van Lieshout
(Netherlands, 1963)

AVL-Ville

Dimensions: various
Client: various
Place of construction: Netherlands
Date of completion: 1998

In 1995 Joep van Lieshout founded Atelier van Lieshout (AVL). One of the many applications that has become AVL's trade mark are the fibreglass constructions in bright, conspicuous colours.
At the moment AVL is building an actual town: AVL-Ville.

Education
1980-1985, Academy of Modern Art, Rotterdam.
1985-1987, Ateliers 1963, Haarlem.
1987, Villa Arson, Nice.

Awards
1992, Prix de Rome Award.
2000, Wilhelmina-ring, Sculpture Award.

Solo Exhibitions (selection)
1988, Galerie Fons Welters, Amsterdam.
1990, Museum Boijmans Van Beuningen, Rotterdam.
1996, Jack Tilton Gallery, New York.
1997, Hausfreund I' Kölnischer Kunstverein, Cologne; Museum Boijmans Van Beuningen, Rotterdam.
1998, The Good, the Bad and the Ugly, Rabastens.
1999, USF Contemporary Art Museum, Tampa, Florida; Museum für Gegenwartskunst, Zürich.
2000, Galerie Fons Welters, Amsterdam.

Commissions (selection)
1990, Ambulatory Bar for the Museum Boijmans Van Beuningen, Rotterdam.
1994, Bars, Sanitairy-units, Wash-stands for Grand Palais, (O.M.A./Rem Koolhaas), Lille.
1995, Mobile Home for the Kröller Müller Museum, Otterlo.
1996, CASTMobiel, CAST, Tilburg.
1997, Clip-On, Centraal Museum, Utrecht (in collaboration with Klaar van der Lippe).
1998, Walker Art Center, the Good, the Bad + the Ugly, Minneapolis.
1999, Sanitairy units, Museum Boijmans Van Beuningen, Rotterdam; Floating Sculpture, Lange Vonder/Twiske Kadoelen, Amsterdam.
2000, Visitor's room Prison Hoogvliet, Rotterdam; Sound reflectors, Luxor theatre, Rotterdam; AVL-Men Sculpture for square in Knokke.

For the Borromini Award Atelier van Lieshout (AVL) would like to submit the large project AVL-Ville. AVL-Ville is a freestate that artist/architect/designer Joep van Lieshout is building for himself and his employees. The purpose is to live and work here self-sufficiently. AVL-Ville has its own flag, constitution and even its own money.

With AVL-Ville Atelier van Lieshout wants to make a beginning for a pseudo-autarkic freestate. Existing laws and expectations are ignored and replaced by self-generated ideas. Everything is based on common sense and result-aimed strategy. In evading certain laws and systems AVL takes control. AVL chooses to replace the word "utopia" , which is no more than an ideal that cannot be realised, by the word "heterotopia" which literally means a place that is different.

Many of the works are linked to each other by a common theme. They are all functional and have a goal of being self-sufficient and independent. For instance the "Pioneer Set", a prefabricated farm that can be assembled and disassembled in any location. All the parts fit inside a 40 ft. shipping container. It consists of a farm house and stables for the animals as well as a chicken coop, rabbit hutches and pig pens. Furthermore AVL made a canteen, a power plant that provides electricity, a city heating system for warm water and heating, and even a field hospital to perform simple operations in. Other objects have an illegal aspect. For instance the weapon workshop: the "Atelier des Armes et des Bombes" or the liquor distillery: the "Atelier de I' Alcool et des Médicaments".

Several concepts to make the works are: Master and Slave units, such as the Mobile Home for Kröller Müller. The slave units are built according to their function, such as sleeping, eating, working. The master unit is the main unit where the slave units can be attached to. They are very flexible and mobile buildings; Skullrooms, such as the Tampa Skull. Skullrooms are small buildings that are shaped according to a function. The space around the human body is minimal. The skulls can be applied as autonomous units or as part of a building; Simple and straightforward constructions. These buildings such as the *Pioneer Set* and the refurbished shipping containers are ungainly but elegant. The material, techniques and production methods are of great influence on the final result.

Other important parts of AVL-Ville are the infra-structural designs. They are machine-like installations. Their industrial character is not denied, but even put forward. For instance the compost toilet that besides its function also gives visual expression to the production and discharge of the faeces.

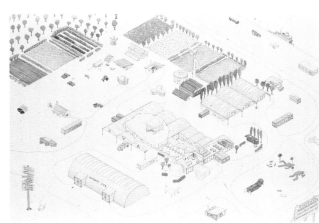

Reason

Intriguing combination
of visual arts
and architecture.
Kristin Feiress

Anna Barbara (Italia, 1968)
Rachaporn Choochuey (Thailandia, 1970)
Stefano Mirti (Italia, 1968)
Akihiro Otsuka (Giappone, 1976)
Luca Poncellini (Italia, 1974)
Andrea Volpe (Italia, 1968)

PC-House

Dimensions: 16 sq.m
Client: Mukojima Net Event
Place of construction: Tokyo, Giappone
Date of completion: 2000

The design and realisation group of the PC-House is formed of individuals of different nationalities and backgrounds. The most important feature of our work is interdisciplinary contamination. We like to mix up art, literature, photography, music and travel in the design process. We're not a firm, we don't have a stable office. Our office is our luggage.

PC-House is a project for a home in polycarbonate built in Tokyo in May, 2000, in occasion of the Mukojima Net Event.

The PC-House is based on the sensorial aspects that derive from the materials used. Architects and designers often concentrate on technology, functionality and the aesthetics of a project tending to forget the sensorial characteristics that are usually a medium for communicating the relationship between technological support, markets and different cultures.

PC-House is a project for a temporary housing unit for two people, 8x2x2 metres in size. The prototype was built by using alveolar polycarbonate technology.

The project derives from closely observing the homeless in Tokyo who live in special cardboard constructions: folding units for one or two persons. It is a somewhat peculiar typology connected to certain cultures and local habits.

PC-House wishes to be the development of a low cost residential system for temporary use that, however, takes into account certain emotional and sensorial characteristics that are often essential and integral in defining the substantial difference between an actual house and a packaging system. This temporary nature is connected to various lines of reasoning. One of these is that in Japan buildings are never built to last forever. Their life is much shorter than the average life-span of a Western building. PC-House can be considered an elementary particle of Nipponese architecture, a possible prototype to be exported and experimented with elsewhere, even in Western countries. Designing a house in Japan (just like living inside it) signifies having to adapt to limited space, using space in different ways, learning new rules, moving within space by following unusual layouts.

PC-HOUSE is a Japanese house for two people where specific choices have been made with respect to the environment, surface area and materials used. It represents a technological challenge to define a new method of contemporary Nipponese living.

In its transparent version, polycarbonate seems to allow an appropriate way to obtain the characteristics of the local housing systems. It represents an optimal solution in terms of privacy, comfort and lightness of interior space. Alveolar polycarbonate, opalescent or transparent, allows a refined lighting system with special effects in terms of texture and surface treatment.

PC-House is created from the unique performance of this material to become a home, an opportunity for innovation and cultural exchange. It also represents a possibility to go beyond shape, fly beyond the domain of emotions and sensations, characteristics that can be explored through the innovative use of materials.

Details

Reason

This is a very subtle project in the way that it merges its physical and sensory qualities. It is also reflective of cultural issues in the frenetic contemporary world, a world which is increasingly characterized by urgent needs and demands which require immediate solutions. This project locates itself in relation to attempts made in the mid-Sixties which were aimed at realizing low-cost building systems and basic living units, in order to respond to the most immediate housing needs.

In this respect, the project raises two interconnected issues, one which relates to the social condition of the homeless in Japanese cities in particular and two, the theoretical context related to the architectural tradition pertaining to these issues.

The use of a polycarbonate material is particularly interesting as it gives the project a sense of cultural awareness, which opens up a possible third interrelated theme. Another significant aspect in the selection of this project is to cite the team of architects, a joint venture which has already worked together on different occasions. The team works as an "interdisciplinary contamination," "an innovative quality that seems to characterize the younger generation of architects, who operate in an undoubtedly contaminated world.
Yorgos Simeoforodis

BlueOfficeArchitecture

Filippo Broggini
(Svizzera, 1961)

Mei-bashi (light bridge)-An-bashi (dark bridge)

Dimensions: 144 sq.m
Client: Daikanyama Redevloment Union
Place of construction: Daikanyama neighbourhood (Shibuya-ku) in Tokyo, Japan
Date of completion: 2000

Founded in 1992 by Filippo Broggini, BlueOfficeArchitecture (BOA) is a small, dynamic structure that aims to be a platform of exchange between industry, engineering, materials sciences, experimentation, and architectural research. For a number of years, BOA has been active in the field of designing and developing footpaths and bridges, and in trialling ultralight structural systems (Alboo®. Aluminium bamboo, Iglhouse®: light compactable housing for tragedy, Pumptensegrity®: inflatable tensegrity systems…) Collaborative efforts with outside offices and research institutions in Switzerland and elsewhere are frequent. Currently in an advanced phase of study are shape-memory living systems (Shape Memory Home ®), ultralight composed beams (Twin Shape Composed Beam ®), and structures for variable-acoustics sound shields.

The footpaths presented here are part of a single design executed and developed between 1997 and 2000 in collaboration with Kajima Corporation (Engineer Kei SUZUKI) for Tokyo's new Daikanyama neighbourhood. The footpaths act as a link between the new residential centre and the Toyoko line underground station. The two footpaths were to define the new limits of the neighbourhood: the northern one (An-bashi) and the southern one (Mei-bashi) – a true entryway to the neighbourhood. In acting in a cultural context outside my own, my aim was to recognize in the objects two elements of opposed qualities, taking inspiration from the Japanese aesthetic principle of "kakushi hagi": strong and weak, black and white, light and dark, sweet and salty, sharp and dull… Both are present, but in different proportions. This way, to my eyes, the two footpaths became metaphors for the "lion" and the "butterfly" in traditional Japanese Kabuki theatre. The first footpath (Mei-bashi) is an airy, light structure, devoted to transparency, even in the arch – a true "butterfly." The second one (An-bashi) is a more massive and cutting structure, a faceted urban beam – the "lion."

The names *Mei* and *An* are in homage to the novel *Meian* by the Japanese writer Sôseki. Technically, the two footpaths' structural system depends on earthquake safety regulations, avoid-

ing supplementary loads on the existing lateral supports. This is why both bridges have central piers and overhanging structure on the two sides. Mei-bashi consists of a suspended trestle with asymmetrical towers and structure, both to signify the interior and exterior of the neighbourhood (a "before" and an "after") and to improve the structure's redundancy. The footpath's lighting comes from the two cantilever arms that light the lower portion of the arch in acidated glass. The light is modulated by blades placed in differing fashion underneath the walking surface.

An-bashi consists of a single body in steel plate (thickness: 10 mm) that acts as a balanced asymmetrical beam. The structure was carried out with technology borrowed from naval construction. To emphasize the dynamics of the structure, a vertical handrail (in compliance with Japanese regulations), inclined with increasing and decreasing logarithmic rhythms, was designed. Lighting is precise both in the upper portion and in the lower portion, to emphasize the faceting of the structure in nighttime hours. These two footpaths are intended to be an example of the search for new fields of interdisciplinary activity (engineer/architect), designed to create new market niches and new stimuli for a profession, that of the architect, undergoing inevitable change.

Reason

Mei-bashi (the light bridge) and An-bashi (the dark bridge), are the two walkways built in collaboration with the Kajima Corporation, that connect the new Daikanyama center with the metro station of the Tokyo Line. Designed in juxtaposition with one another, they are poetically founded on the strong and powerful image of the lion and on the airy and light image of the butterfly, both historical symbols of the Kabuki Theater. The project successfully blends structural contents, strongly conditioned by anti-seismic needs and by regulations and standards, with clear symbolic and communicative meanings, overcoming the traditionalism between engineering and architecture.
Livio Sacchi

Daniel Bonilla
(Colombia, 1962)

Colombian Pavilion-EXPO 2000

Dimensions: 1400 sq.m
Client: Colombian Government
Place of construction: Hannover, Germany
Date of completion: 2000

Architect graduated from the University of Los Andes (1986-Bogotá) and Master of Arts in Urban Design from Oxford Brookes University (1990-UK). Further studies have also been acomplished at The College of Technology in Dublin and the Milan Polytechnic. As Architect and Urban Designer worked for the Public Space Bureau in the Local Authority Central Offices of Bogotá (1986-1989), and also in the London based office of Llewelyn-Davies for two years starting in 1991. After returning to Bogotá he worked as the Design Director of Ospinas y Cia, a major development company in Colombia. In 1997 he set formally his own practice as Daniel Bonilla, Architecture and Urbanism, where work has focused mainly on architectural design of any kind of buildings together with projects concerning public spaces. The diversity of commissions have mostly been obtained by enrolling public open competitions, such as the commission for the design of the Colombian Expo-2000 Pavilion. Other winning entries have been the Design for Street Furniture for Bogotá, Major Square in Pasto City, Police Station in Armenia. Other many awards have been obtained in several competitions. In simple terms, the work developed at his practice is concerned with a careful exploration on space and architectural form and its dynamic relationship, no matter how much is built or unbuilt in a particular project, but always keeping in mind the idea of moving one step forward in terms constructive solutions, image and time.

It is the first time that Colombia participates in a world exposition with its own building. The pavilion design was selected in an open and public competition with seventy one entries, where we as architects concluded that considering the major effort that Colombia was doing to participate in Expo Hannover, we should provide a solution that would be a sample of modesty in the Expo by designing an economic and simple building, rather than pretending to be the most impressive or spectacular building of the Expo. The pavilion's architecture represents the Colombian jungles, with the use of a geometrically arranged group of trees with a technological language, interpreting figuratively and in a contemporary way the country's natural resources. Under this structure appears an open area that evokes the loquacious living in the streets and squares of our country, full of activity, where trade takes place and where people are able to contemplate and listen; enriched with different light intensities, a variety of sounds, lots of aromas and textures. This preamble that plays a strong role in the EXPO's street activity, is an invitation to enter a calm interior that has plain images and seeks to seed questions in the foreigner who crosses quickly throw this little piece of Colombia. Additionally and as companion, a quiet volume which reuses simple orthogonal containers, shines giving place to the private and administrative activities.

Technically the whole has been harmonized with the inclusion of passive systems that optimize the energetic and light consumption, the heat, the ventilation and by the implementation of recycling systems, the exploitation of the basic resources. This pavilion which is one of the most economic within the EXPO in terms of construction, establishes its supportability in the fact that is a totally prefabricated building that is able to be risen in six weeks and can be rebuild in its totality in any other geographical place of Germany. This means that there is a 100% exploitation of resources, only possible thanks to a very strict modularity and to the simple, few, easy to transport and to mount pieces that compose the building. The materials used are basically the "teca" wood, cultivated in the Colombian coasts in a vanguard and exemplar project, together with a metallic structure that obeys in its totality to the requirements and normative of the European community. This building proves at the end how resourceful Colombians are, and how much capable and peeper we are to be a part of the cultural and intellectual elite of the world.

Roof details

Reason

This pavilion proposes a solution that beautifully expresses the characteristics of the culture that it represents. The design of the pavilion is an example of humble, simple and inexpensive design. The use of simple, natural materials in the construction of the pavilion expresses a certain essence of the country of Colombia. While this may seem to be an obvious reference to the construction techniques used in this country, it is however a profound reference to the reality of the building systems available in a developing country. The pavilion clearly expresses these concepts without overpowering the surrounding pavilions. But that is not all. The design goes beyond a mere formal response to the problem at hand, in that the project exhibits a respect for natural resources, an issue which ideally should be considered in every architectural project. In this project, the pavilion incorporates recycled materials, utilises natural ventilation and conserves electrical consumption.
Camilo Salazar

Alessandro Bucci
(Italy, 1964)

Area Cimatti

Dimensions: 3900 sq.m
Client: CMC Faenza
Place of constructions: Faenza
Date of competition: 1999

Graduated in architecture in 1991 in Florence, Supervising Professor Adolfo Natalini. In 1992, he attended the post-graduate specialization course in "Architectural applied designing" (OIKOS UNIVERSITY). Since 1993 he has been a professional free-lance architect as a member of the "Cooprogetto" studio in Faenza. From 1995 to 1998 he was a Member of the Building Commission of the Town of Faenza. Since 1993, he has been an instructor at the Faculty of Architecture in Ferrara (Architectural composition held by Prof. Arch. Massimo Carmassi) and is presently a contract professor of the 4th year, 2nd Designing Course.

The project area is located along the borders of Faenza's historical center, directly in contact with the remains of the ancient walls that surrounded the Durbecco Borgo and opens out onto a large park, in an ideal position for a high quality unit that restores urban value to an area that has been degraded. The project aims at restoring and enhancing the value of the buildings, reproposing the importance of the existing street, restoring the image of the interior protected courtyard, separating pedestrian walkways, bicycle paths and roads and their connection to the already existing ones, highlighting the ancient plant which is the project's generating center. The project volume is divided into three bodies, two having a residential nature and the third with a daytime center for the elderly and protected residence.

The interior residential building will have four floors above the ground; the building along the main street, three floors crossed by a central opening on the ground floor that constitutes the princi-

pal pedestrian entrance into the compound and into the park. The center for the elderly will include three mini-apartments on the first floor and a day-time center on the ground floor whose main access will be highlighted by a metallic pergola linked with the common areas, enlarging the surface area available during the summer months. Since the very beginning, the objective has been to create an actual urban structure that can transform the user's social variety into the project's strong point. The various households, the elderly that will permanently live in the protected residence and those who will simply use the services offered by the day-time center, do not live in separate situations, but find various possibilities of meeting and exchange in the courtyard – the center of the compound – created by the conformation of the buildings: the functions are integrated with one another following the logic of adding different shapes, both for what concerns the proposed uses, as well as the management of the compound.

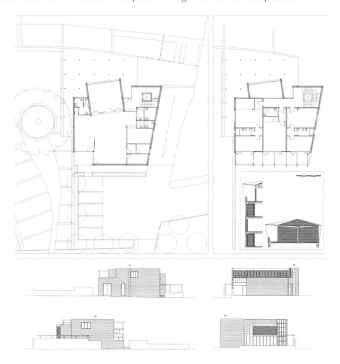

General view and details
of the other building

Reason

This is an interesting example of social housing. The complex acts to help define the urban public spaces at the edge of the historical centre of the town of Faenza.
Mirko Zardini

Javier Hernando Castañeda Acero
(Colombia, 1967)
Luis Guillermo Hernández Vásquez
(Colombia, 1964)
Carlos Mario Rodríguez Osorio
(Colombia, 1968)
Mauricio Alberto Valencia Correa
(Colombia, 1967)

School of architecture and design
(Pontificia Bolivariana)

Dimensions: 2900 sq.m
Client: Universidad Pontificia Bolivariana
Place of completion: Medellin, Colombia
Date of completion: 1999

Javier Hernando Castañeda Acero Teacher at UPB
and National University.
Luis Guillermo Hernández Vásquez Teacher at UPB
and National University.
Carlos Mario Rodríguez Osorio Teacher at UPB.
Mauricio Alberto Valencia Correa Teacher at UPB.

Awards and Distinctions
2000, XVII Colombian Biennial. Honorary Mention
Antioquia Arquitecture Award Caribbean Cultural Park,
Barranquilla, Competition, Second Prize.
1999, 4th International Architectural Biennial of São
Paulo, Brasil, Ex Aequo Award.
1998, Antioquia Architectural Award Medellin University
Graduate Center, Competition First Prize Ferrini School,
Medellín Competition First Prize.
1998, Medellin Metro Restaurant, Competition, First
Prize.
1998, Itagüí Civic Center, Competition, First Prize.

Exhibitions
2000, Leopoldo Rother Architectural Museum, National
University of Colombia, Bogotá. 2000, La Tertulia
Modern Art Museum of Cali, New Colombian
Architecture.

Horizontal and vertical movement, are actions that occur in any architecture, but that can also be its guiding principle, the purpose of a project. In fact, we believe that the School of Architecture and Design extension is the product of an expression that states "Architecture is learned in the school's hallways". There would not be another way of explaining the project but from understanding it as a point of encounter, a place for discussion, and for the exhibition of works, those matters which give meaning to an Architecture and Design School.

These are not the building's brief, but they define the best way to inhabit it. The project, connected with the existing circulation structures, is planned as an academic scenery which is integrated with its horizontal and vertical circulation patterns. These are tensioned as its ends by the project's singular components (auditorium and exhibition room) and are always in relation with the "awards" patio, which could previously only be seen through the windows. The determination to create an intermediate space between the patio and the studios, is responsible for the risk taken in facing the studios to the street and in the planning of the circulation patterns – both horizontal and vertical, which broaden and grow narrow.

General view and park
facade

Reason

In this work by Castañeda, Hernandez, Rodriguez and Valencia, one can clearly see the search for originality and architectural identity utilising past experience. The design of the building is the result of a clear concept that is uniquely materialised in the composition of the architectural elements. The various spaces of the building are organised in tandem with a play of architectural volumes that contribute to a satisfying architectural experience. The concern for the overall design ideas are evident in all details of the building. This is fully carried out in the symbolic meaning of interior spaces: the corridor, the stairway, the student meeting areas are in fact generators of the entire spatial sequence.
Camilo Salazar

Alfonso Cendron
(Italy, 1960)

Joint Ownership Villa
(ten low-cost homes)

Dimensions: 1000 sq.m
Client: ATER TV
Place of construction: Roncade, Veneto, Italy.
Date of completion: 1995

Graduated at IUAV in 1986, where he taught and carried out research. He implemented projects and competitions as of 1987, for which he received awards and recommendations (Cosenza, 1996; IN/ARCH-Domus, 1997; Pirano, 1998; Oderzo, 1999; Cosenza, 2000). He collaborated with Gregotti Associati and was consultant to the United Nations. In 1994, he established CENDRON STUDIO with Beatrice Ciruzzi (who was born in Castelfranco V. in 1964), in which Renato Da Vico (who was born in Milan in 1966), Diego Fabris (who was born in Treviso in 1967) and Leonardo Torresan (who was born in Treviso in 1969) also collaborate.

Bibliography
V. Gregotti, Six Projects in Italy in "Casabella", no. 629, December 1995.
E. Cosano, Joint Ownership Villa in "Incontri sulla Giovane Architettura Europea", Seville 1996,
F. Irace, Award for First Opera in "Domus Extra 1997".
M. Mulazzani, Socialofts, in "Almanacco di Casabella 1998-1999", september 1999.
A. Campo Baeza (essay), *Socialofts*, in "Giovani Architetti Europei", Clean, Napoli, 2000

The contract for designing the project was awarded following the "Call for bids for a public residential building contract" implemented by ATER in 1990 for the ENEL area in Porta Carlo Alberto in Treviso.

The project involved experimentation to reduce the figurative aspect of a rented house into a unitary system. The architectural form of the Joint Ownership Villa is the same size as the surrounding buildings. The idea was to provide the building with a central cavity comprising a portico facing onto two courtyards, which derives from the traditional farmyards in ancient farms in the Po Plains area.

The building has a longitudinal axis and three ordinary transversal axes, acting as both horizontal and vertical connecting axes, structural axes, visual axes and light axes. A separator is placed along the central transversal axis of the building to act as the structural and technological organizer. A double system of "optic corridors" along the north-south perimeter comprises verandas to provide light, ventilation and vision.

The openings in the day sections of the homes are also located along the north-south face passing through the courtyards in order to ensue the apartments always face both north and south, the road and the courtyard or the courtyard and the garden.

The building is in block form and comprises three main parts: the first faces east and contains four two-people apartments on the ground and first floors, two five-people duplexes on the second floor facing west, and four three and five-people duplexes on the third floor, which is suspended between the two previous floors.

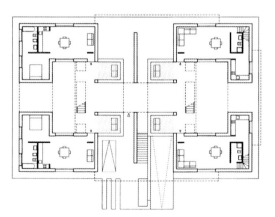

General view

The internal courtyard
and the passage

Reason

Remarkably well
proportioned and cleverly
scaled building. Very
accomplished, simple
detailing unpretentious.
Interesting inner spaces.
Offers good promise
for Italian architecture.
Ross Jenner

Davide Cristofani
(Italy, 1964)
Gabriele Lelli
(Italy, 1964)

The "Villa Azzurra" Psychiatric Hospital and Outpatients Department

Dimensions: 7000 sq.m.
Client: Villa Azzurra S.p.A.
Place of construction: Riolo Terme, Italy
Date of completion: 1999

Both graduated in architecture from Florence in 1991 (Supervisor Adolfo Natalini). They established the Fabbrica di Architettura (Factory of Architecture) in 1992. They teach at the Faculty of Architecture in Ferrara, where G. Lelli is Professor of Architectural Composition, and at the IUAV in Venice where Lelli collaborated with Massimo Carmassi. They won the ANDIL 2000 "First Work Prize" with their project for Villa Azzurra in Riolo Terme and received a special mention at the Luigi Cosenza European Prize for Architecture 2000. They are currently working on the Santa Lucia residential complex in Imola, restoration of Palazzo Zucchini in Faenza and the P.P. in Via Salvemini in Faenza. They have been published in Casabella magazine, Young Italian Architects, The Almanac of Italian Architecture, 1997-1998, 1998-1999 and 1999-2000 editions.

This hospital proposes an experimental environment for the cure of mental illnesses. Following the "Basaglia Law", psychiatric illnesses are treated without isolating patients from the outside world. When a patient specifically requires hospitalisation, the "distance" between this particular environment and domestic influences become the typological context of the building. If the distance is too great, isolation increases, as in a typical hospital, however if this distance is too minimal, the environment becomes overly permeable and ineffective. The experimental "distance" in this project emulates a grand hotel, which means reception, service and freedom to build one's own temporary domestic environment.

Costarella: this building is located near the bath town of Riolo Terme, and was built and operates in relation to the sloping area and surrounding landscape. The natural terrace is called the "Costarella" and, together with its oak trees, is the heart of the system of levels on which this new hospital was built. The blocks constructed closer to the hill are protected and introverted with traditional openings to provide hospitalisation with a domestic connotation.

On the other hand, the daytime areas in the light and transparent building located on the lower terrace open to the outside, by means of large verandas overlooking the Senio Valley, and are protected by a wood and metal brise-soleil. At the foot of the two main buildings – on the Costarella Terrace – flexible blocks outline the fluid space of the general service area, comprising entrance, offices, cafeteria and auditorium.

Interior and exterior: Due to the delicate relationship with the exterior, and in order to define the spaces, parallel elements have been used rather than a fence, thereby allowing the landscape to freely cross the premises and creating perennially open spaces. The interior areas are very different from one another and are arranged along intersecting axes which overlook particular sections of the landscape.

Serenity: the outdoor areas are created horizontally using simple and neutral forms, rather than dynamic ones, which are strongly fixed to the ground. Weights are transmitted perceptively according to the principle of trilith to generate a sense of security and avoid potentially anxious conditions. The relationship with matter is direct and authentic, using few materials that are both traditional and recognizable.

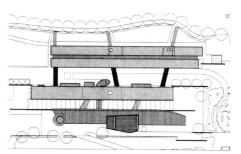

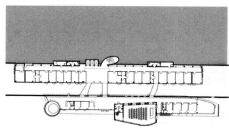

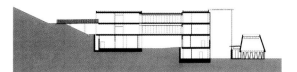

Transversal section

General view

The portical and
the waiting room

Reason

I write for the purpose of nominating Davide Cristofani and Gabriele Lelli Architetti, (La Fabbrica di Architettura), specifically for the Specialized Center for Mental Illness, "Villa Azzurra", Riolo Terme, completed 1999. Lelli and Cristofani are young architects who have completed a number of medium scale buildings, each exhibiting a sensitivity to materials, scale and site. They work within established modernist languages, but they find moments to moderate and re-calibrate these know strategies. Hence they innovate within a tradition rather than starting from scratch. The results are always clear, precise, and sympathetic. The Specialized Center for Mental Illness, "Villa Azzurra", Riolo Terme is a building that takes these established themes to a higher state of refinement. The inside and outside are integrated through views, framing, and enveloping scrims or trellises. The emphasis on the horizontal weds the building to its site. The strict boundary of interior and exterior is blurred through formal devices as well as detailing strategies. The structure of the program is clearly reflected in the relationship of "introverted" spaces, protected by the hill, and the collective spaces, which are airy and open. The use of light is especially important. Light is used to define forms, but it is also modulated and controlled to give variety and underline programmatic differences. The architects use traditional materials with grace and delicacy. They never disguise the nature of the materials, or the means of construction. In this way they make the experience of the building open to its future inhabitants. This is a building that needs to be seen in the context of an unfolding career, showing a process of continuing development and refinement. Its innovations are incremental, but their cumulative result can be significant.
Stan Allen

The project presents a new idea and new elements for a psychiatric structure. The building proposes a new type of relationship with the countryside and plays on the contrast among materials to elegantly define the different main parts of the buildings.
Mirko Zardini

Without reason.
Alberto Campo-Baeza

Design Office

George Yu
(USA, 1964)
Jason King
(USA, 1966)

Design Office 2

Dimensions: approx. 38 sq.m
Place of construction: Culver City, California, USA
Client: Design Office
Date of completion: December 1999

George Yu B.A., M.Arch., Registered Architect Principal
George Yu received a Bachelor of Arts degree in Urban Geography in 1985 from the University of British Columbia and Master of Architecture degree from the University of California in Los Angeles in 1988. He has taught design at the Southern California Institute of Architecture, the University of California Los Angeles, the University of British Columbia, and the University of Texas, Austin. His work has been featured in I.D., Azure, Parachute, Insite and Architectural Record and exhibited at the Ottawa Art Gallery and the Los Angeles Municipal Art Gallery. He has received two I.D. Magazine Design Distinction Awards and honors from the Architectural Foundation of Los Angeles. Yu was awarded the Canada Council's most prestigious award in architecture, the Prix de Rome, for 2000.

Jason King B.Arch., M.Arch., Principal
Jason King attended the University of British Columbia and earned a Bachelor of Architecture (Honours) degree from the University of Toronto in 1991 and a Master of Architecture degree from Harvard University in 1996. He has taught architectural design at the University of British Columbia, Harvard University's Graduate School of Design, the Boston Architectural Center, the University of Texas, Austin and the University of Kentucky where he was the Sue Fan Gooding Visiting Professor for 1998. Jason's work has been featured in Azure, Trace Magazine, I.D. Magazine, and Architectural Record and has been exhibited at the Workscene Gallery in Toronto and the Van Allen Institute in New York. He has received the Canada Council Arts Grant in Architecture, I.D. Magazine's Design Distinction Award and the Canada Council's most prestigious award in architecture, the Prix de Rome, for 2000.

The Design Office 2 studio project is a new office building that we have designed and are building to accommodate the rapid expansion of our company.

In addition to trying to design an interesting environment that is conducive to working for long hours in a very concentrated manner, it is also a vehicle through which to explore issues of "temporality" (it is constructed of building components and systems that can be demounted and reconstructed as required) as well as low budget construction and the utilization of recycled materials.

The design/build process involved a variable and open ended method that allowed for design and detail changes based on previous phases of construction or newly obtained or recycled materials.

General scheme

1. 1 1/2" corrugated metal decking
2. 1/2" sandblosted glass
3. 1/2" lexon thermoclear panels
4. 1"x 1" steel angle frame
5. 1"x 1" steel tube frame
6. laminated plywood door
7. 2" diameter steel tube speedrail frame
8. 3/4" plywood floor
9. concrete block foudation
10. 2 x 8 wood platform framing

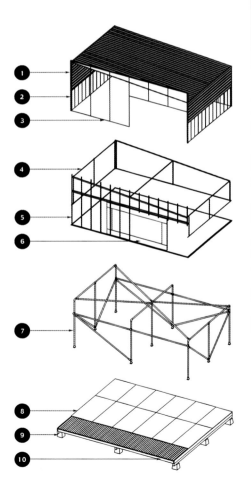

Details

Reason

The Design Office 2 studio is of interest for both its intrinsic and external qualities. Designed and constructed by DO (Design Office) for itself, this new building is far from being a mere glamorous object waiting to be published in Wallpaper as part of a so-called "world wide architectural hype". It was thought of by its designers as a "vehicle through which to explore issues of *temporality*" as well as being an economic response, thanks to a tight budget (about 15$ per sq.ft) and the use of recycled materials. Above all, its construction consciously takes note of its environment and the landscape. All these characteristics are quite atypical in the Californian – and more particularly LA's context. In a place where fashion, image and high technology dominate (including the work and clients of DO), this project appears to me as a silent manifesto mixing aesthetics and – do I dare? – ethics. Architectural practices often need to expand temporarily. Instead of doing it with urgency, why not think about it and provide an efficient though pleasant and thoughtful solution. That is exactly what DO has done with its new office building.
Didier Fiuza Faustino

Isabelle Devin
(France, 1962)
Catherine Rannou
(France, 1964)

The Garden of the Dunes
and the Garden of the Winds

Dimensions: 6000 sq.m
Commission: Children's playground
Place of construction: Paris-Park de la Villette
Date of completion: 1998

Isabelle Devin and Catherine Rannou started to work together at the international competition Europan 1. They won the first prize for their "brackets" project, an attempt of phantasmagorical flats in the chinks of the city. Following this competition, they created their studio in Paris in 90. The Ministry of the French Equipment supports their research by publishing (editing) their *Album de la Jeune Architecture*, the AFFA and the Ministry of Foreign Affairs awarded them a research grant on the children of Sarajevo. Their main realizations are: "The Garden of dunes and winds" in the Park of Villette in Paris, the refitting of the IRCAM in Paris (architect R. Piano) and the playful spaces of the Park du Grand Marais in Amiens (landscape painters: G. Clément and G. Geoffroy Dechaumes). At the same time they participate in competitions and carried out projects situated in parks and gardens: Jardin d'Acclimatation, Jardin des Tuileries, Zoo de to Paris, Parc Astérix, Parc du Château de Versailles, Center Parcs Hollande. Teachers at the Superior National School of the Landscape of Versailles.

Exhibition
Museum of Modern Art of the city of Paris, Centres Georges Pompidou in Paris; Gallery Aedes in Berlin.

A maritime and playful atmosphere creates dynamic wanderings along wave-like dunes.

In this garden the wind is the unpredictable actor. Children can feel the wind and its unpredictable breath, measuring themselves against it, through sails, inflatable mattresses, windmills, "kite-lamps", and parasols.

The landscape serves both as a support for the games and their stimulus. The children bounce on rubber floors and air mattresses, they climb on the walls made of pebbles, pedal to activate the windmills, and turn around in hamster wheels.

All the elements: the games of ladders, the textures, the vegetation, movement, atmosphere, and the visual and auditory stimuli, contribute to create a scene arousing feelings that create an emotional attachment, a bonding to the space, and a sense of well-being.

A dialogue is created between their bodies and the landscape. They discover that there can exist in the city a space of holiday and relaxation, a break from their routine. A space is created in which the person is involved both experientially, emotionally, and as an active participant.

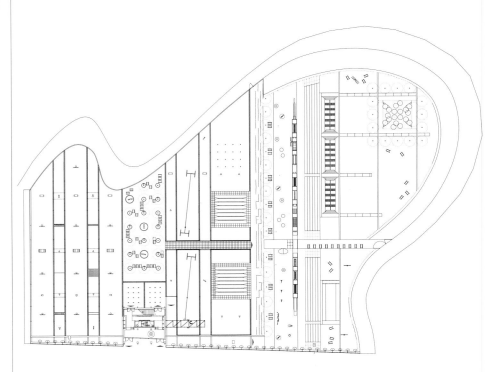

General plan

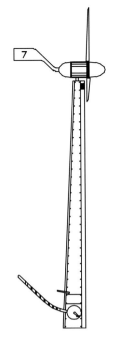

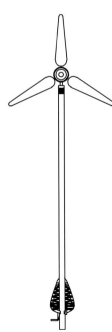

The dunes and the winds:
details

The garden

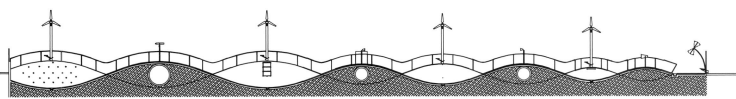

Longitudinal section and
detail of the mobile wheel

Reason

Not only have all
the standards and
requirements for
children's spaces been
met, but the limits of
function and habit have
also been surpassed to
reach new conceptual,
spatial and environmental
horizons in a vital
interaction with the
location and with man.
Akram El Magdoub

dRMM

Alex de Rijke
(UK, 1960)
Philip Marsh
(UK, 1966)
Sadie Mogan
(UK, 1969)

Moshi Moshi Brighton

Dimensions: 196 sq.m
Client: Moshi Moshi Sushi
Place of construction: Brighton, UK
Date of completion: 2000

dRMM was established in 1995 by Alex de Rijke, Philip Marsh and Sadie Morgan. The practice has taught at the Royal College of Art, University of London Bartlett, and they now teach at the Architectural Association. The work is diverse in both scale and construction. Much of it has been won through competition and are at various states of completion, such as a central-government funded project for a secondary school, landscape proposals for an inner-city market, entrance and offices for Selfridges, and the recently completed Architect's Registration Board. The practice has recently been short-listed from an international field of competitors for the regeneration of the South Bank Centre. dRMM's first new building a restaurant in Brighton, has been short-listed for a RIBA Civic Trust Award and has been critically acclaimed.

Brief & site: Moshi Moshi introduced the sushi conveyor-belt concept to England with three restaurants in London, and for 2000 approached several well known architects with an idea for a restaurant at the Bartholomew Square site. The competition brief called for a response which embodied Japanese culture, improved commercial viability of the existing pavilion, increased seating capacity and enlivened the square.

Cultural context: Brighton is a seaside town with architecture of hedonism, spectacle, and in the case of the Piers and Pavilion, extremes. The combination of the sea with a certain sophistication, whether fashion, music or food continues to lure Londoners, tourists and Labour Party delegates alike. In a small town where eating out is the primary industry, opening yet another restaurant can be a gamble. Successive former bar/cafes on the site had all failed.

Architectural context: Bartholomew Square is officially the Town Square, with the 1980's Council Offices forming two sides, on the third the large concrete Thistle Hotel, which blocks any view to the sea. The 19C Town Hall, a large square block, rescues the square from corporate anonymity by forming the fourth side and entrance to the square with an imposing stucco classical set piece.

Existing pavilion: in the middle of this bleak square stood "The Pudding Bowl" a forlorn neo-Victorian octagonal domed structure of sub-Nash detail, a contemporary to the 80's hotel/office developments. This "pavilion" in the square set the tone of pretended jolliness on a surface of petrol station paviours. The Planning Authority were, after an initial refusal, open to the radically different proposal.

Design approach: the Town Hall portico and it's corner connection to the "lanes", the intimate small scale of shops and restaurants adjacent, formed the architectural context to which we responded with an uncompromisingly modern construction. We decided to superimpose a new and larger orthogonal structure onto the existing octagonal foundations. The route across the square to the sea exit from the lanes enters the building on a diagonal, a movement line we developed.

Concept: our winning proposal illuminated the square with a simple 14x14x3.5 m³ light box apparently hovering over an extended raised deck. This can also be read as a delicate "lantern", like those found in Japanese temple gardens, but in this case at an urban scale strongly contrasting with the mass

of the Town Hall. A smaller intersecting solid box contains the service requirement of kitchen, toilets and storage. A simple 'garden' of beach pebbles and mobile bamboo trees define the site limits.

Materials: glass, Kalwall fibreglass, resin, sheet copper, softwood decking, fluorescent paint.

Construction: the construction of the pavilion is unique in that a prefabricated lightweight enclosure of translucent fibreglass with a 'skirting' of clear glass is suspended from a steel frame such that the whole facade can slide off and open up to the square. This technical feat was developed with Kalwall & MHA engineers, installed by Guildprime Shopfitting to dRMM's detail. A 6.5 m square plywood & copper roof, supported on unframed glass forms a large cruciform lantern in the crimson ceiling. Underfloor heating and tungsten lighting provides discreet warmth with intimacy.

Inside out: in any weather the restaurant can open to reveal the interior as an exterior to the curious passer-by, the sliding facade becoming a free-standing screen in the square. There is no visible track, no threshold in the decking, no framing to the glass or glazed doors, no clues to the servicing or separation of the materials. This helps to enlarge the scale and enhance the external/internal ambiguity.

The contemporary shoji reference of the "moving wall" enables an interesting interchange between public and private; a variable dialogue between the table, the snaking 42 m conveyor belt of sushi, and the stone garden and town itself entering the interior.

Conclusion: most elements of the building were carefully selected from catalogues. The only special fabrication requirement was the stainless steel conveyor belt, detailed to span 8m lengths and change levels. The pendant lights and all furniture were designed by dRMM to coordinate with other materials and cut costs with a reduced palette.

The Opticon building plays a Zen-like game of scale, light, materiality and transformation on a shoestring budget of £ 250,000 excluding catering equipment.

This approach to design exactly corresponds with dRMM's methodology; the judicious use of economic standard components to create a non-standard architecture of maximum performance. Customers are showing their appreciation in droves, with enthusiasm for the freshness of both sushi and architecture.

The interiors

Night view

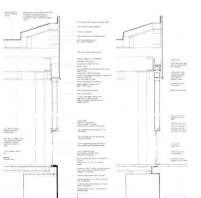

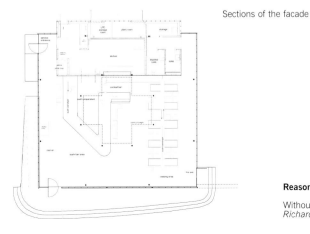

Sections of the facade

Reason

Without reason.
Richard Burdett

FIELD Consultants

Michael Markham
(Australia 1960)
Peter Brew
(Australia, 1964)

The Holyoake Cottage

Dimensions: 125 sq.m
Client: Catriona Holyoake
Place of construction: Hawthorne, Melbourne, Australia
Date of completion: 2000

1994 Founded by Peter Brew & Michael Markham FIELD Consultants has for the past 7 years executed works ranging from low-cost houses and public toilets through to car lots and interiors. Occasionally the partners write and lecture.

Awards
1994 Architecture Australia Unbuilt Work Prize
2000 Royal Australian Institute of Architects.
Victorian Chapter Awards.
The Victorian Architecture Medal.
The Harold Desbrowe Annear Award.

Publications
1997, *Local Heroes*, AR Australia 60.
1997, *Bandstand. City Square*, UME 5.
1999, *Architecture for Another Nation*, Monument 28.
2000,*Holyoake Cottage*, Architect-Awards Issue.
2000, *Field Day*, AR Australia 73.

The Holyoake Cottage received the top award in the residential category, The Harold Desbrowe-Annear Award, and for the best building overall, the Victorian Architecture Medal at the Royal Australian Institute of Architects, Victorian Chapter, 2000 Awards.

"The Holyoake Cottage is a modestly sized family home. Virtually every aspect of its design suggests an alternative way of dealing with the house but also, by implication, rethinking an approach to architecture generally. The house was typically Victorian: dense with intellectual content and supported by its ghosted homages to the history of domestic architecture in Australia, to the Griffins, to Grounds, also to Bill and Ruth Lucas' own house in Sydney, but also to the tradition of invention in the post-war years in the hands of the Smithsons... the house as an unfinished experiment in living. Confounding orthodox expectations, everything about this house suggests the obverse of the normal, a roof that holds water and does not shed it (for water discharge delay and summer cooling), walls that are doors (for variable use of internal/external relationships), a back door that is a front door, a monumental rear elevation made of translucent plastic, an attic bedroom at kids scale on the ground floor. Here is a Case Study House: a proposition for what is possible." (Jury Comment Extract)

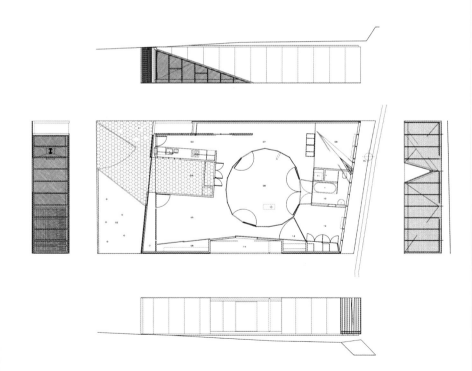

The main front on the hill

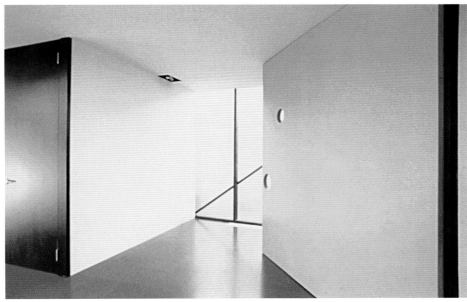

Reason

Field Consultants (Michael Markham & Peter Brew) have come to distinguish themselves by a few works that are mostly modest in scale and comparatively inconspicuous but which are exemplary in the way they push the boundaries of the discipline in experimentation and invention. In their hands the question of dwelling becomes something of a demonstration model. Like Case Study Houses, their domestic works are a proposition of what is possible in minimal, detached, spatially and energy efficient single family houses. They continue the cultural legacy of Walter Burley Griffin and the modernist Roy Grounds in interpreting the needs of the collective life in a New World context and of the worker's cottage in the 19th Century city (as their bandstand project, for central Melbourne, restates the site of the earlier cultural collective). Everything in their work confounds orthodox expectations, suggesting the obverse of the normal, for example, in the Holyoake Cottage the roof holds water, the rear elevation is monumental but riven by a tree, the rear rooms are attic-like but single storied, the traditional veranda is defined by sliding metal screens. The central courtyard, reminiscent of the music room of Asplund's Snellman villa forms a sort of interior nature for the song of birds. All accommodation is as a series of cupboards with large doors rather than walled rooms. Even the car is stored like an appliance. Suspended, the works never claim their sites but are conceived as a gift to the city and to nature.
Ross Jenner

Toni Gironés
(Spain, 1965)

Passanelles

Dimensions: 1600 sq.m
Client: pubblic
Place of construction: Cadaqués, Girona, Spain
Date of completion: 1995

Main Projects
2001, 26 Homes (old industrial warehouse), Badalona.
1999-2000, CoAC Exhibition, Girona.
1999-01, Detached House, Collbató.
1999, Flower Patio, "Girona, flower time".
1998-2001, Industrial Warehouse, Cervelló.
1996-2000, Promenade, Cadaqués.
1996-2000, Servicing Basin (Natural Park - Creus Cape).
1995-2000, "Passanelles", Cadaqués.
1995: CoAC -BCN Exhibition.
1993-1994, Book-publishing store (Montgat).

Competitions and Awards
2001, II European Landscape Biennial.
2001, N-II Code. Badalona. Limited Competition.
2000, Experimental Homes, "Forum 2004", BCN.
2000, Swimming Pools, Raval -Bcn.
2000, IBERFAD Award
1999, Civic Centre, St Quirze di Safaja.
1998, Architecture Awards, Girona.
1998, FAD Award.
1996, "UIA 96" under 40 Award,

Teaching/Research
2000, Design/Planning Professor.(ETSAV-UPC). BCN.
1999, Ph. D. Thesis: "Spontaneous Architectures: Observations on Architectural Constant Elements".
1996, Speaker, "Cinema and Architecture". UIA 96-CCCB. BCN.
1995-1999, Member of "BCN Metàpolis".
1994-1997, Ph. D. Courses (ETSAB). BCN.

This project stems for the concept of "unit", stone unit = stone = "passanella" (local name) = a slate flat stone, which can be found in the area where the Pyrenees touch the Mediterranean, on the Creus Cape tableland, more precisely, near Cadaqués.

Cadaqués: a sea-town, connected to the rest of the community via one single path, which encloses the town in a sort of "cul-de-sac" (one single route, both to enter and to leave the town, which is thus isolated, and takes the shape of a circle). The village is defended and surrounded by the "Panì" mountain, where it appears with its two clean-cut facades.

Getting to the beach a throwing a "passanella" (a stone), trying to bounce it and make it slide on the water, is a day-to-day activity, here.

The project is based upon this action, and upon the will to interpret the place as a complete, multidimensional reality.

The work develops over a liquid, dynamic, and changing landscape: the sea, but only when it is smooth – "ses minves" (the low tides in January).

The work is divided into:
– a static part: floating elements (buoys);
– a dynamic part: ephemeral traces left by the stones.

The buoys are placed into the water with a regular design, over a 40x40 m surface. The result is a board consisting of ten 4-meter-wide and 40-meter-long channels; the horizon is used as the reference at infinity. Another eight 5-meter channels are laid in the opposite direction. We can now draw an imaginary staff, establishing a relation with the acoustic vertical and horizontal lines (music).

VERTICAL = TONE = stone DISTANCE
HORIZONTAL = TIME = stone BOUNDS

The sum of the various series of throws leads to an acoustic record (melody)... of the infinite lines and tunes that this "game" can compose.

At the end, still on the beach, a computer will interpret the landscape recorded during the entire performance.

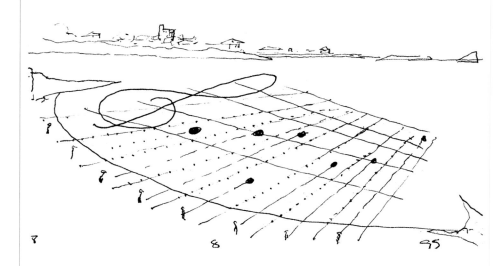

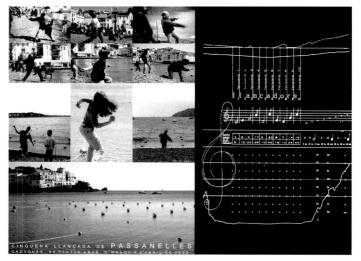

The space and
the performance

Reason

This work is
recommended because
it is an original, playful
project of landscape
architecture: a plain
temporary installation
in the sea, a modern
interpretation of ancient
popular traditions. It has
been set up for three
consecutive years, thus
becoming a festive
recurrence, which reflects
the place's identity.
Franco Zagari

Marco Graber
(Switzerland, 1962)
Thomas Pulver
(Switzerland, 1962)

School for apprentices, Berne

Dimensions: 4000 sq.m
Client: City of Berne
Place of construction: Berne
Date of completion: 2000

They made their diploma at ETH/Zurich in 1989. In 1990 and 1991 they were collaborators in the studios of Cruz & Ortiz (Seville) and Torres & Martinez-Lapena (Barcelone). In 1992 they founded their own studio in Berne and Zurich and today the have a team of 6 collaborators. During the last years they taught as assistants and lecturers at the ETH in Zurich and the FHZ in Winterthur. Marco Graber and Thomas Pulver have won various competitions in the last 8 years, the building for the school for apprentices in Berne is the first project they could realize. Different competition projects have been published and discussed in professional journals and they have been member of "Treffpunkt Barcelona" a group of young Swiss architects who have spent a certain time of their professional background in Barcelona.

The conversion of an old spinning mill near Berne into a school for apprentices called for the construction of an entrance block housing laboratories, offices, a computer room and the new main entrance for the hole building complex.

The design by Marco Graber and Thomas Pulver won a competition held in 1995: it presents a volume with rendered outer walls while its sculptural force is accentuated by slender but highly effective slits in the exterior which provide apertures for the illumination of the interior and enhance its rapport with the exterior of the building. The slit in the main facade, for instance, stresses the entrance and creates space for an opening in the floor which illuminates the rooms below. A similar slit separates the rear of the building from the volume of the spinning mill and creates further sources of light. The visual relationship between the new part and the old is established by a great window in the lobby, furnishing a view out over the interminable sequence of roofs of the spinning mill.

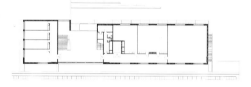

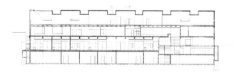

The main entrance
and the stairs

Reason

A "simple" building of a surprising complexity: due to its position and its architectural intensity it is clearly the new main building of several lateral buildings added to the huge shed hall the former spinning will, which therefore is not questioned to remain the centre and the heart of the whole complex; the form of the building and its openings interact precisely and effective with the urban situation and topography; the varying structural systems on the different levels of the building are used to create a variety of spaces with different characters. With the new shed construction in the neighbourhood of the ancient production hall an adequate form for the training workshops of a professional school is found: half classroom, half workshop; interesting and beautiful hall and corridors; exemplary collaboration of the architects with the artist Elisabeth Arpagaus: the result of the concept of colors and materials worked out together is surprising and of a striking beauty. It is an inseparable part of architecture as a whole; first important construction of an architectural office that, in competitions, had made several important contributions to the architectural discourse in Switzerland, mainly in the field of urbanism.
Martin Tschanz

Grego & Smolenicky

Jasmin Grego
(Switzerland, 1964)
Joseph Smolenicky
(Switzerland, 1960)

Accenture
(Former Andersen Consulting)

Dimensions: 2100 sq.m
Client: Accenture (former Andersen Consulting)
Place of construction: Zurich, Switzerland
Date of completion: 1999

2001, First prize, competition Casino Theater, Winterthur.
2001, Strozzi's Bar, Zürich.
2000, First prize competition Louis Häfliger park, Zürich.
2000, lecturing in Winterthur, Luzern, Zürich.
2000, prize winner, Swiss Federal Scholarship of the Arts.
2000, First prize, competition Hotel Neuhaus, Interlaken.
2000, First prize, competition Headoffice Accenture, Frankfurt, Germany.
Restaurant Kornhauskeller, Bern.
1999, First prize Hochparterre and Swiss Federal Television, for best Bar/Restaurant of Switzerland.
1999, Central Bar Café, Zürich.
1999, First prize, Headquarters Schweiz Accenture, Zürich.
1998, Poolbar SYLT, Zürich.
1998, Study Entrance building Zoo, Zurich.
1997, Planning for Shopping Center Lochergut, Zürich.
1997, Case study dwellings Melchrüti, Wallisellen.
1997, Competition addition Kunsthaus, Aarau.
1996, Project Dancefloors Opernhaus, Zürich.
1996, Holiday houses, Misox.
1996, Lecture Architekturforum, Zürich.
1995, ZELO elected most beautiful hair dresser salon of Europe.
1995, 2. prize, competition, administration building Jockey, Uster.
1995, Communication agencyVIVA AG, Zürich.
1993, Villa am Niederhofenrain 11, Zürich.
1993, Competition for Berlin as Cultural Capital of Europe
(Exhibition).
1992, Hair dresser salon Zelo, Zürich.
1992, Competition for Paris as Cultural Capital of Europe
(Exhibition).
1992, Prizewinner competition Swiss Pavillion Sevilla.
1992, Studio Grego & Smolenicky is founded.

Floor plan strategy: the offices of Accenture occupy two floors of a famous neoclassical building in the centre of Zurich, facing the river on one side and situated on one of the most exclusive business and commercial addresses of the city on the other .

In order to do justice to these two very attractive, though very different urban qualities we have developed a plan in the shape of the Janishead with two entrances. These two entrances contain the volume and each acts as the beginning and end of a sequence of movement.

The different typologies of workplaces find their own location appropriate to their special character and needs in the differentiated parts of the plan: small, enclosed offices for concentrated, independent work look down from the galleries - the café, a space for informal encounters, is placed at the interface of all traffic, with a marvellous view towards the river and the historic town.

Atmospheric intentions: the offices of Accenture (former Andersen Consulting) are used by the constantly travelling members of the company as a non territorial workplace equipped with many services, much like a first class hotel.

We wanted to create a pleasant, institutional home for these modern nomads. The image of an English "Gentlemen's' club" became the central atmospheric notion. It captures the idea of a certain exclusivity, the feeling of "being at home" wherever in the world – a place to meet like minded colleagues in an atmosphere of general well-being for social and professional activities.

Many elements of the project originate from residential interiors, like table lamps, curtains, carpets, textiles in general. Technology is understood as a self-evident, highly developed and omnipresent but invisible and at all means discreet servant. It is never used as a formal or atmospheric inspiration.

Architectonic painting: due to a previous renovation we were confronted with a difficult situation with a very general and unspecific character. A crucial point of the project was the removal of a series of steel galleries, in order to restore the room to its original height. The spaces, however, remained soulless.

The idea of "architectonic painting" was developed as a means of confronting a problem resulting from the fact that after the previous renovation the construction works were considered finished.

We designed "paintings" on the walls that were not intended to portray any artistic content, but to serve architectonic purposes, such as, defining directions, proportions, axiality, and monumentality. They were designed to be a cultural hint to real works of art without being art themselves.

This idea of creating spatial and atmospheric structures through the "paintings" is directly connected with the neo-classical exterior of the building, thus creating a dialogue between the interior and the exterior.

The degree of abstraction in these "paintings", and in all the furniture and interior elements is connected to the reduced material expression and the lack of details in the wall and ceiling surfaces we had found in the existing spaces.

What results is an ambivalent oscillation between an almost historic expression and a world of completely sober and abstract form. The tension created between the large degree of artificiality and the realistic concrete allusion was of great interest to us. Our ideas about things and their effective visibility tend to differ in this matter. Perception seems to fool us here, our imagination is at least as real as the physical presence of the things themselves.

A meeting room

The main entrance and
the waiting room

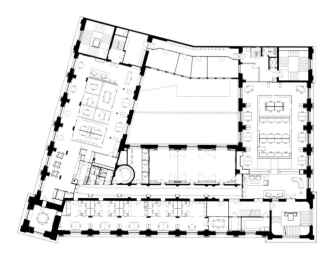

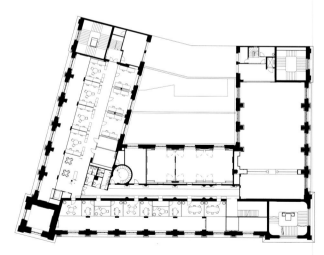

The main floors

The working place

Reason

G&S propose a differentiated architecture for our highly differentiated world. They do not aspire to a uniformity of personal language, but instead to a broadly informed synergetic instrument with which they believe architecture sustains its reality. Recognizing in architectural and urban reality the true physical manifestation of the actual condition of the man-made world, they acknowledge and accept its conditions: contradictory, complex and unique.

They claim that historic presences that have passed the test of time remain strong in a contemporary context and are able to correspond and participate in today's criteria.

Accepting and incorporating multiple contradictory demands, G&S's project always establish new interrelations between the world and its vast array of architectural vocabularies, inevitably re-creating their own, uniquely meaningful order. Each of G&S's projects, as if from the hand of another author, is newly original in its manifestation. Authorship itself is no longer a central theme. It exists and is recognizable only in terms of a general architectural position. Architecture is thus liberated from the individual signature and donated to the shared contemporary and historical plurality.

Their dream is an architectural philosophy in which not only the plan, urban typology, proportion and materiality are discussed, but also where the issue of Form is positioned within the bounds of precise criteria; not mythologised through amateurish and ill-defined argument.

Jacqueline Burckhardt

Greg Lynn
(Usa, 1964)

Korean Presbyterian Church

Dimensions: 20.000 sq.m
Client: Korean Presbyterian Church
Place of construction: New York, USA
Date of completion: 1999

Greg Lynn has taught throughout the United States and Europe and is presently the "Professor of Spatial Conception and Exploration" at the ETH in Zürich, the "Davenport Visiting Professor" at Yale University and a "Studio Professor" at the University of California Los Angeles. His office Greg Lynn FORM is working in collaborative partnerships with a variety of architects and designers on a range of projects including: the Uniserve Corporate Headquarters (Los Angeles); Transformation of the Klieburg block in the Bijlmermeer (Amsterdam); a line of international showrooms for PGLIFE.COM (Stockholm); the Cincinnati Country Day School (Ohio); the Vision Plan for Rutgers University (New Brunswick, NJ); an aluminum book container design for Visionaire Magazine nr. 34; and the recently completed Korean Presbyterian Church of New York (New York City). His work has been exhibited internationally in both architecture and art museums and galleries. The most provocative are his collaborations with the painter Fabian Marcaccio for "The Tingler" at the Secession Museum in Vienna and "The Predator" at the Wexner Center in Columbus, Ohio. He and his UCLA students represented the United States in the American Pavilion at the 7th International Exhibition of Architecture at the Venice Biennale, where his own work was also featured in the Italian and Austrian pavilions. He is the author of several books including: *Animate FORM* (1999), *Folds, Bodies and Blobs: Collected Essays* (1998) and *Embryological House* (forthcoming spring of 2001). He was born on the 7th of September 1964. He graduated cum laude from Miami University of Ohio in 1986 with two degrees, one in Philosophy (B.Phil.) the other in Environmental Design (B.E.D.). He graduated from Princeton University with a Master's of Architecture (M.Arch.) degree in 1988.

A 210,000 square foot project including the addition to and renovation of the previously abandoned Knickerbocker Laundry factory, built in 1936. The factory's industrial vocabulary is retained and manipulated to facilitate a unique confluence of cultural programming for the primarily Korean American congregation, including a 2500 seat church and multiple non-sectarian programs such as an 80 classroom school, a 600 seat wedding chapel, various assembly spaces, a choir rehearsal space, a cafeteria, a library and a daycare center. "The sanctuary is the most impressive interior in New York in many years." "Is as striking as those we once had to go to Los Angeles to see." Herbert Muschamp of the N.Y. Times.

The new location for the Presbyterian Church of New York in Sunnyside, Queens, is the collaborative effort of Douglas Garofalo, Greg Lynn and Michael McInturf involving the adaptive re-use of and addition to an existing factory building. The design team worked in three cities; Garofalo Architects in Chicago, Greg Lynn FORM in Hoboken (now Los Angeles), and Michael McInturf Architects in Cincinnati. Through internet connection, the combined offices could assemble over a twelve person team that exchanged CAD files, model photos and other project information throughout the typical day. By distributing the workload variably between offices and with the combination of each office's experience and expertise, the three small offices were able to design a project that would have been too large and complex for any of them to manage individually. The existing building, originally the Knickerbocker Laundry Factory, designed by Irving

Fenichel, was built in 1932. The 88,000 square foot factory building was originally constructed as a two story laundry facility with 15' clear height ceilings and a large three story boiler room to provide power. In 1932, it was described by the architectural and cultural critic, Lewis Mumford, as America's best example of "misplaced monumentality" due to its South facade.

This monumental, deco inspired facade of precast concrete was built to exploit the visibility of the site from the Long Island Railway tracks. The architectural approach to the re-use of the factory building as a church was to retain the industrial vocabulary of the existing building and transform its interior spaces and exterior massing into a new kind of religious building. Its scale and industrial vocabulary reflect the importance and uniqueness of the church congregation. The form of the addition exploits the eccentricities of the existing structure which is divided into roughly two areas; the first is a large shed structure with repetitive, long span, open areas; the second structural system of steel elements to the South vary greatly in length, depth and orientation. The addition relates to these existing areas through two types of construction; the first is a long span shed structure that is clad in metal and has an undulating shape following the rail lines; the second set of forms are stucco-clad entry tubes which snake between existing structural bays vertically through the building. Where the existing building presents a vertical facade to the railway the new building sets up a much more horizontal relationship to the site with this combination of low undulating forms.

The main hall and details
of the construction

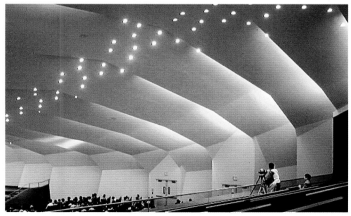

Reason

His theoretical work
is of greatest importance,
as his use of computer
programmes to create a
new type of architecture.
Kristin Feireiss

M&T, Müller & Truniger Architekten

Andreas E. Müller
(Switzerland, 1964)
Daniel Truniger
(Switzerland, 1965)

Town Hall in Jona

Dimensions: 3365 sq.m
Client: Town of Jona, st.Gallen
Place of construction: Jona, St.Gallen, Switzerland
Date of completion: 1998

The two partners, Andreas E. Müller and Daniel Truniger, began their collaboration during their studies at the Swiss Federal Institute of Technology ETH in Zuerich. After their studies, they were assistants at the Institute for Spacerepresentation and Spacegrasping (New media experiments in Architecture) with Prof. Rudolf Manz at the ETH in Zürich.
The beginning of their business work was marked by the First price at the Competition for a new Town Hall in Jona, Switzerland.
Recently, M&T worked on a Childrens Zoo on Private Housing Projects and on several competitions (i.e. the competition for an additional wing to the Swiss National Museum; invitation to the 2nd level of the competition). M&T develop appropriate buildings and tectonic structures; controverse, timeless, compelling.

Publications
Hochparterre, nr. 1-2, 1999, Evelin C. Frisch, "Ein Hôtel de Ville in Jona"
NZZ, 6-7 Februar 1999, Roderick Hönig, "'Steinernes Jona'"
SI+A, nr. 7, 19 Februar 1999, Martin Tschanz, "Der Tradition verpflichtet"
Archithese, nr. 1, 1999, Peter Omachen, "Eine neue Generation"
Bauwelt, nr. 13, April 1999, Theresia Gürtler-Berger, "Ein Haus für Besucher"
Bilanz Spezial, Bauen & Wohnen, Mai 2000
Hochparterre, nr. 10, 2000, Ulrike Schettler

Lectures
"Erstlingswerke"; Swiss Federal Institute of Technology ETH Lehrstuhl Kollhoff; 1998
"Müller & Truniger, Zürich"; "Young Swiss Arcitects" Architektur Forum Zürich; 1999
"Z um Beispiel Berlin"; Discussion Forum, Volkshochschule Rapperswil; 1999
"Über Kargkeit"; Fachhochschule Lippe, Detmold (D); 1999

Prizes
Nomination for "Best Of Switzerland 98" Competition (Hochparterre, 10 vor 10)

The Town Hall is a house for visitors. The task of building a Town House in this particular place demands a unique statement – it bears the possibility of reforming the heart of a municipality. In the past years the town of Jona has become a city. The construction of the Town Hall sets an urban standard, by which future developments will be judged.

The compact body of the new building joins other existing single buildings consisting of the church, the schoolhouse and the community-centre. These four architectural focal points form the gravitational centre of the urban community. In this context the new Town Hall assumes the duty of a complex representative public building.

The community centre obtains its image from the urban context and implants it into Jona. The building defines its space; it represents without becoming arrogant. It is open and inviting and it is a house for the public. The building completes the line of the main street and opens an appropriately sized area off of its western side. Here the building stands – a self-confident protagonist – at the central crossing.

In the east, the building defines the schoolhouse court. A quiet place is created, the atmosphere of which is determined by a large pool at ground level.

The horizontal structure of the elevation is divided into the base, a centre section and the roof. Vertically it shows a narrow grid with emphasis on the corners. Exceptions in the strict grid form the main entrance and large panoramic windows at the north and south elevation. These windows light a longitudinal hall, that extends as a multi-story sequence throughout the building.

The building's exterior is a solid volume of grey limestone. This stone comes from a quarry on the grounds of the community; the house is built with the stone on which the community stands. The raw surface of the blocks react to changing light and weather conditions. The anodised window wings and the dark frames make for a distinguished elegance. The quartzite of the base finds continuity as an interior flooring material.

Visitors enter the building by means of a low entrance area and find themselves in the two-story lobby. A broad staircase leads into the hall on the first floor. Here a large window opens one's view to the alps. Further stairs lead to the upper area of the hall, where another window frames the image of the roofs of the township and the nearby hills.

This hall area is the heart of the house. Its organization was inspired by visitor-oriented buildings such as theatres, museums or libraries. Its hybrid space determines the house. According to the public function of the hall, the proportions and materials of the walls correspond to the external facade.

In general the hall is the communication centre and rest zone and on special occasions it changes into a showroom or an event area.

The clarity of the proportions and the selection of suggestive materials underline the representative purpose. The use of stone in a massive construction, the exquisite woodwork, the accuracy of the details and the delicate colour palette determine the building.

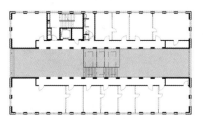

Tipical floor and
longitudinal section

The main opening outside
and from the interior

Reason

A single volume, situated
carefully in the urban
fabric. A house, not just
a building: built of local
stone, with a base and
a roof, it retains the
memory of a traditional
house, but with its regular
façade it articulates also
its function as a modern
administrative building.
The typology is an
innovative reinterpretation
of a traditional town hall
with an inner courtyard:
a public hall connects
the three public floors.
Meandering through the
building, one is aware
of its largely horizontal
orientation. This is partly
due to the two large
windows at both ends
of the building that open
it up to the city.
The materials used
and the articulation
of the architecture are
of a certain dignity,
appropriate to the
building's programme.
Inside the house a precise
hierarchy of spaces is
established.
Jona is a community in
the periphery: it is formed
of several former villages
around the little city
of Rapperswil, which
however is not part of it.
It is situated on the upper
end of lake Zurich, at the
outskirts of the urban area
of Zurich. Its identity was
quite weak: several
shopping areas could be
thought to be its centre.
The new town hall is
situated at an important
crossing, in the
neighbourhood of other
public buildings. It is
a true "Hotel de ville":
a house of a certain
strength and dignity, and
it in fact has become
an important element
of identification for the
community.
The town hall of Jona
is the first important
building by Muller +
Truniger. In recent
buildings and projects
they make clear, their
willingness to adapt their
architectural language
to a specific building
programme and situation.
For the elephant pen
in a children's zoo they
created an almost
organic and very joyful
architecture, quite
different from the town
hall of Jona.
Martin Tschanz

The main stair: general
view and details

Meeting room

Mathew & Ghosh Architects

Nisha Mathew Gosh
(India, 1969)
Soumitro Ghosh
(India, 1967)

White Walls and Light
(House for Mary Mathew)

Dimensions: 236 sq.m
Client: Mary Mathew
Place of construction: Bangalore, India
Date of completion: 1996

Architects Nisha Mathew Ghosh and Soumitro Ghosh graduated from the School of Architecture, Ahmedabad, India in 1994. Now living, teaching and working from Bangalore since 1995: they are involved in doing educational, industrial, corporate, religious, residential buildings and interiors. Central to the practice is the search for a critical, contemporary solution to each project in the context of narrowing borders of the world and the visible specificity of the conditions of each project. The negotiation between the abstract universal and the specific aspects of design and building continue to enrich the design process through projects built/unbuilt. The path of practice and teaching has oriented the architects to a way of seeing, thinking and making of architecture.

In search of the essence of dwelling in the contemporary context, this house is interpreted as a conceptual relationship of parts. A coming together of form (the south west captive wall excludes heat, creating deep light striations on the white walls and scooping in breeze) and space (the garden-court and the verandah – a spatial archetype brought into a position of confrontation by translocating it from the street or periphery to the center and between the garden courts. Reinterpreting the contemporary urban family life (with its impermanence's, and shifting boundaries yet being aware of the deeply etched cultural spaces of a people). The act of redefinition desires to restore man's relationship with nature in the ambiguous context of an urban metropolis like Bangalore (the slow severing of which has already begun).

Sandwiched between two larger plots, this dwelling abuts the road on its 30 feet front and goes in 85 feet deep. The building makes the first formal gesture by the creation of a "thick wall" along the southwest; that is perceived along the main road approach to the house. The porous configuration is realized as a sequence of spaces only upon entering the house.

The natural environment integrates with the main living spaces, which are in the nature of a deep verandah attached to the garden court. The programme is developed around these primary spaces – the verandah and the "garden-court".

The garden-court is formally defined as the focus by the water tank's pivotal position at its corner. The verandah is flanked by the southwest wall, which in differing 'densities' encloses the service spaces and shields the garden court from the sun.

The private chambers revolve around the garden court accessed through a sequence of a gallery on the ground and the study on the upper level as transition. The structural system of parallel load bearing walls, jack arch roof slab with reinforced precast cement concrete beams and pre-cast hollow terracotta tile panels with minimal reinforcement was chosen. It became a directive for the articulation of spaces, fenestrations, interior surface and exterior façade. The details inside complement the nature of spaces. Bands of stucco on the slab and beam edges articulate the otherwise bare exposed wire cut brick wall exterior.

In the gentle-harsh light characteristic of temperate Bangalore the surfaces are luminous in white, rising from a floor of terracotta tiles and an in-situ gray cement continuous band around the periphery of the spaces, this gently mediates between and separates the horizontal plane from the vertical.

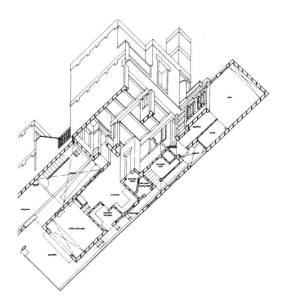

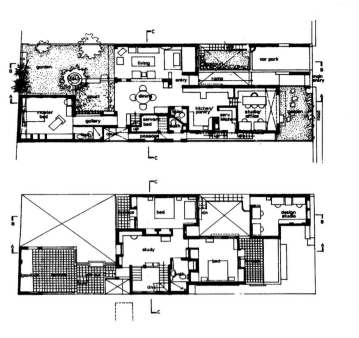

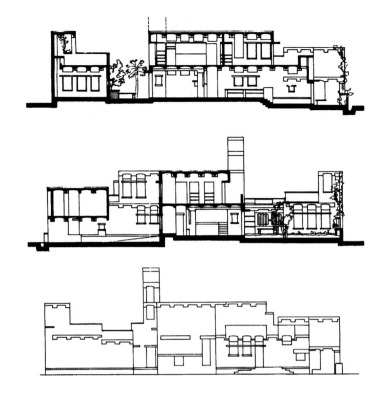

Ground and first floor.
Longitudinal and
transversal sections

Reason

The new dynamisms
of India, and the sub-
continent, which is
mobile as never
before on the economic,
industrial, political and
military fronts. Cities are
in a frenzy responding
to conflicting desires, in
a state of decomposition,
transition and metastasis.
Its vast outsides/protective
membranes gone,
Architecture must secure
a new footing now. It
can no longer dwell
in its habitual comforts,
nor on academic
and theoretic alibis.
Mathew and Ghosh's
practice operates by
obtaining the 'map'.

Available in their design
process via alterations
and meditation. This is a
mapping of the secret
places – the wishes – one
senses in the architectural
process as it unfolds.
They perceive, and in
their perceiving, stabilise.
The aim is in
conservation, not in the
sense of preserving
buildings, rather of
preserving a history,
specifically a history
of experiencing.
Evident is their
determination to resist
the common affliction, a
compulsion to side with
presiding powers. Mathew
and Ghosh do not
emulate, their practice
does not become the
instrument – or 'media' –
conveying the interests of
status bearers. Prevailing
cannons of taste and
consumption have no
place here. One sees well-
established solutions,
techniques and aesthetics
at work. Always driven
towards new questions.
This is a necessary
economy here in the
South. There is a great
sense of authenticity and
affirmation of the desire
of this practice to come
on its own.
Anand Bhatt

181

njiric + njiric arhitekti

Helena Njiric
(Croatia, 1963)
Hrvoje Njiric
(Croatia, 1960)

Both graduated from the Architectural Faculty, University of Zagreb. Until 1990 worked in several offices in Zagreb. 1990-1995, free-lance architects in Graz. Since 1996 own office in Zagreb.
Visiting critics at the HAB Weimar, the ETSAB Barcelona, the TU Wien, the AA School of Architecture London, the ETH Zuerich and the Strathclyde University of Glasgow. Unit masters of international workshops in Amsterdam, Zagreb, Merano, Maribor, Gorizia, Barcelona and Brescia. 1997-2000, appointed member and chairman of Diploma Committee – prof. Joost Meuwissen at the TU Graz. 1998-1999, visiting professor (Entwerfen 3) at the TU Graz. 1999, assistant lecturer at School of Architecture in Zagreb (Helena Njiric). 2000, visiting professor at Facolta di Architettura – Ferrara (Hrvoje Njiric). 2000, visiting professor at TU Ljubljana (Hrvoje Njiric). 2000-2001, guest lecturer at AF Zagreb (Helena Njiric). 2000-2005, professor for Building Typologies and Housing at TU Graz (Hrvoje Njiric).
Winners of several awards and international competitions: Den Bosch (1993), Schwerin (1993), Graz (1994), Glasgow (1996) and Maribor (1996).
The work of the practice has been the subject of various exhibitions – in Graz, Berlin, Rotterdam, Ljubljana, Vienna, Glasgow, London, Leeds, Rome, Sofia, Edinburgh, Newcastle, Copenhagen, Orléans, Maribor, Weimar, Piran, Madrid and Zagreb. Currently shown in de Singel gallery in Antwerpen and it will be published by ACTAR (Barcelona) in summer 2001.
Built work: Baumaxx Hypermarket (Maribor), McDonalds Drive-In (Maribor), House B (Slano) and House N (Zagreb) in preparation.

Baumaxx Hypermarket

An urban concept of reversing the figure/ground ratio of american hypermarkets. A celebration of traffic, performed by cutting the regular parking patterns into the irregular plot contour, should be strenghtened by the green roof substance, as a new elevated ground, publicly accessible. The negative reaction of developer turned the former concept into the new perceptual reality – *no trespassing*. The landscape is thus to be observed/mentally, consumed/remote-controlled. The surreal nature of fireplace on the roof terrace of de Bestégui appartment by L-C is equaled by the virtual status of the landscaped zone in the Hypermarket.

All inward-bound planes are entirely glazed, all perimeter ones are mute, but user-friendly. A green roof as a common denominator and recreated artificial topography. Four billboards "anchor" the vast slopes of the House to the site and turn to the traffic streams. Color "classification" is an attempt to handle architecture by ordinary, if not banal, criteria – size, smell or color. By assigning *colour*, as a consumption-profiled term to the projects, we are trying to *resume* the manifold facets and secret ambitions of every single one to an understandable and communicative platform, but also not to limit ourselves with a couple *sizes*. On the contrary, different shades of a single colour, could transmit even subtle expectations of particular design.

We think of a house in its natural appearance: wood is wood, brick is brick, concrete is concrete. Even the glazed elevations from the first façade concept exploited the properties of insulating wool as such. We used its yellowness as a part of the Baumaxx corporate identity, attaching simply the red logos onto it and blurring them slightly with corrugated polycarbonate sheets. Color as a marketing strategy. In the theory of visual communications yellow and red are considered as "cheap", low-budget colours. That is why such D-I-Y markets use them.

Finally, the client rejected the solution in favour of prefab concrete panels. In order not to loose the impact of "active" elevations, it was decided to remain in the *realm of ready-mades* by choosing to put a layer of custom-made traffic reflectors in signal red and silver atop of concrete. The op-art effect is addressed to the drivers as major circulation force on the spot. Such a kinetic experience of the envelope – silver from the north, red from the south, neutral from the west, blends with the firm's corporate colours. In the night the House turns to the pure Light.

Immediately after completion, the Slovenes "discovered" unparalleled similarity with the oeuvre of The Father. What came out of necessity to resolve the tensions of the site and objectives of the program, was suddenly seen as a blasphemous remake of Plecnik (the Church of The Holy Heart, Prague 1933). Should a comparable design – in overall layout and formulation of the skin, really be prosecuted? Although we had never considered it as referential to our project, the hints put forward by the high priests of the Plecnik religion, made us think. Isn't a temple of christianity the right typological ancestor for the house of contemporary religion – that of consume? What are parallels like – entrance Baumaxx panel / statue of St Mary over main doors, or bell-tower / billboard, but a document of shifted social concerns – from the spiritual to the material? Could the Venturi-like semiotics testify of the similar system of signifiers, appropriated for the masses?

Dimensions: 12.500 sq.m
Client: KR Karlheinz Essl, Schoemer AG
Place of construction: Maribor, Slovenia
Date of completion: 1999

Longitudinal section

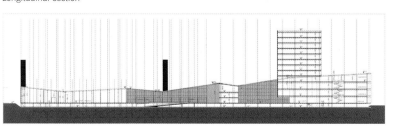

Study sketches

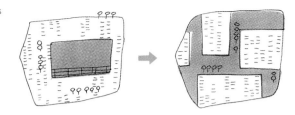

The main facade

The roof

Reason

On the actual international level njiric + njiric belong to one of the most interesting teams, regarding to their innovative lucidity and precision, their clarity and positivistic optimism. After many winning competition- and other projects, this shopping mall is their first big realization. The ground idea is an Urban concept of reversing the figure/ground ratio of American hypermarkets. A celebration of traffic, performed by cutting the regular parking patterns into the irregular plot contour, should be strengthened by the green roof substance, as a new elevated ground, publicly accessible. The negative reaction of developer turned the former concept into the new perceptual reality – *no trespassing*.

The landscape is thus to be observed/mentally, consumed/remote-controlled. The surreal nature of fireplace on the roof terrace of de Bestégui apartment by L-C is equalled by the virtual status of the landscaped zone in the Hypermarket. All inward-bound planes are entirely glazed, all perimeter ones are mute, but user-friendly. A green roof acts as a common denominator and recreated artificial topography. Four billboards "anchor" the vast slopes of the House to the site and turn to the traffic streams. The perimeter walls are made of prefab concrete panels. In order to give them the impact of "active" elevations, it was decided to remain in the *realm of ready-mades* by choosing to put a layer of custom-made traffic reflectors in signal red and silver atop of concrete. The pop-art effect is addressed to the drivers as major circulation force on the spot. Such a kinetic experience of the envelope – silver from the north, red from the south, neutral from the west, blends with the firm's corporate colours. In the night the House turns to the pure Light.
Miha Desman

OCEAN north

Kivi Sotaama
(Finland, 1971)
Michael Hensel
(Germany, 1965)

OCEAN north is a non-commercial multidisciplinary organisation of architects, urban designers, and industrial designers. The group was formed in 1998 by Kivi Sotamaa and Michael Hensel and is located in Helsinki, Oslo and London. The organisation assumed its non-commercial structure with the aim to liberate itself from predominant economic dictates and therefore to maintain maximum freedom in pursuing a critical research agenda as an alternative to mainstream production. This research agenda is rooted in an approach to design that focuses on instrumental methods of yielding new spatio-temporal paradigms of relational dynamics between material form and social arrangements. The portfolio of OCEAN north includes design and research in the following fields:

Design
Urban Design, Building Design, Interior Design, Furniture & Product Design, Exhibition Design, Installation Design, Stage Design, Multimedia Events;

Research
Time-based Methods and Processes in Design, Advanced Digital Technology in Design, Alternative Urban Design Strategies and Methodologies;

Dissemination
Academic Engagements, Conferences & Symposia, Publications.

The Intencities Pavilion

Dimensions: Unlimited - from Object to Building
Client: Various
Place of construction: Helsinki, Finland
Date of completion: 2000

It was designed as part of the Helsinki Cultural Capital 2000 events. The site for the intervention was Makasiini a 19th century u-shaped and single storey block of ex-railway depots, facing the Finnish House of Parliament and Kiasma - Stephen Holl's Museum of Modern Art. The aim of the intervention was to further pursue the research into the design of dynamic environments - established by Chamberworks and Ambient Amplifiers - by means of broadening the scope of involved conditions and elements and thus to achieve a richer pallet of interactions. The intervention incorporated elements of art, architecture, dance, music, media, and graphic design.

The multi-disciplinary design team formulated an approach of a loosely coupled choreographic layout in order to engender dynamic interactions between scheduled performances, defined formal, sonic, tactile, and material elements and emergent flows of movement and ambient effects and across the site. The architectural component of the intervention featured 5 geometrically differentiated structures made of steel tube, veneer, and plastic film. Each structure consisted of a partly surfaced wire-frame-like substructure. While the structures provided for occupational arrangements, such as stages, seating or circulation areas, viewing platforms and bridges, none of these provisions were evident from their geometric articulation. Not unlike the Extraterrain project these surfaces revealed their occupational potential only through unfolding events and performances.

The utilisation of these surfaces was not prescribed, but emanated from their spontaneous activation by the performers, visitors and audiences. The construction and surfacing of the structures was distributed over time, changing their appearance and presence in the site over time. Motion triggered light and sound systems were integrated into the structures and enabled a dynamic relation between the visitors and the changing ambient effects of the intervention. In acting as projection surface the structures configured an audio-visually animated landscape as well as both stage and backdrop for the different performances of the intervention. The introduction of new media technology served to translate real life movement within the site into digital environments, which were projected onto the material surfaces of the 5 structures. A unique concept of interaction allowed the visitors to use both their actual movement and their mobile phones to manipulate the projected graphics and therefore the entire audio-visual appearance of the intervention. The dance performances evolved randomly in relation to visitor movement and participation.

The initial distance and distinction between the dancers and the audience was gradually eroded when the dancers moved through and with the audience. In doing so the initial social arrangement was reversed and yielded participation of visitors in the performances. Surface painting activities were linked with the dance performance on the one hand and the visitor's movement on the other hand. Tracing the various movements of dancers and visitors, the painter created layer upon layer of traces. At times the painter became integral part of the dance performance, at other times he randomly followed the movements of visitors, light intensities, density of media projections, or sound impulses. In this way the differentiated geometry of the material construct, the changing intensities of ambient effects, as well as the individual and collective movement of visitors and performers continually converged and diverged, provisionally assembling and dispersing the elements of the intervention.

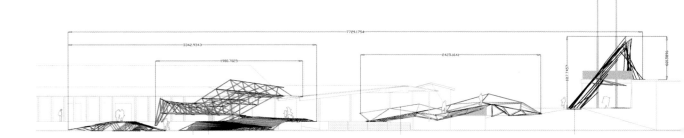

Reason

In the spirit of collaboration that Borromini often found himself forced to undertake, I am nominating OCEAN north, a noncommerical group of architects and designers that pursues research in design. Formed in 1998 by Kivi Sotamaa, Michael Hensel, and Johan Bettum (who has since departed), OCEAN north has outposts in Helsinki, Oslo, and London. I am nominating OCEAN north not for a single building but for the construct of their collaboration: a cross-cultural group formed to liberate the architects from the dominating economic dictates of practice and to give them the freedom to pursue a critical research agenda as an alternative to mainstream production.

This is an important and risky step for young architects to take, and one that merits close attention. Rather than rush into building without understanding the always changing social and economic environments that challenge designers, OCEAN north has begun with imaginative and successful exhibition and furniture design and the occasional competition, like their provocative and fantastic Töölö Open Arena project. Combined with research into "fields of ambiguity" and "event envelopes," OCEAN north has already shown their potential to eclipse the work of Aalto in the 21st century. This is an exciting network whose great promise deserves serious consideration for the Borromini Young Architects Award.
Cynthia C. Davidson

Po.D

Cho Hyoungjin (Coree, 1966)
Raoul Adrien (France, 1972)
Feghali Remi (Lebanon, 1974)
Heng WhooKiat (Singapore, 1976)
Sidirahal Lofti (Morocco, 1979)
Benarroch Michael (Israel, 1978)
Berrada Mehdi (Morocco, 1976)

Po.D is an association that is the brainchild of three projects themed "urban mutation" produced in the architecture studio under professor Odile Decq at Ecole Spéciale d'Architecture.
The emergence of new technologies in the lifestyle of urban nomads, which we are evolving into in our cities at the beginning of this century, pushed us to engage in an experimental research: what will become of the space-time relationship between the contemporary individual and his or her immediate environment (urban, natural, social...)? The physical reality of our trade (urbanization, architecture, design) interests us as much as virtual reality (cyberspace, virtual networks of communication...)

iNSTANT eGO

Dimensions: 1,6 m³
Client: Mass produced wearable architectures for general consumption
Place of construction: Rèro (S.A.) workshops, Groslay, Ile-de-France, France
Date of completion: 1999

In the city, Antoine Picon introduces cyborgs that roam in the urban territory with a constantly growing speed. Interruption time, non-time is thus multiplied and made inevitable. Our nomadic space is then both the result and the reason of these intersticial durations allowing the emergence of intimate space in the middle of the urban public space. Plugged to our clothing, iNSTANT eGO is primarily a cluster of intelligent tissue folded over, waiting to be unfolded.

When released, the interface unfolds, subjective time is trapped in our personal space, creating an ambiguous space-time relationship where other people's time is only subject to our personal intimate time. Space is transformed by its own kinematics, headed towards the time "zero", where telecommunication is the main source of pictural and lingual information: thinking, writing, refreshing ourselves, we are capable of achieving our most intimate gestures. This plugable and flexible space interacts only indirectly with its close environment. Parametrable, iNSTANT eGO is sensually related to the local context, transmitting its energy flows, its virtual potentiality.

A dress to be lived: axonometries and sections

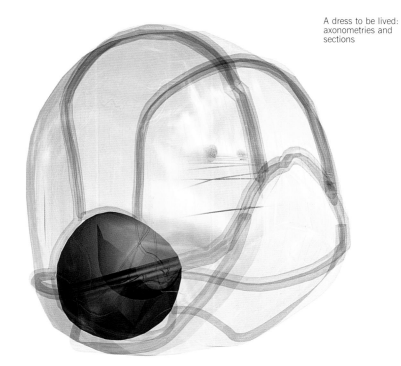

iNSTANT eGO is an intimate, nomad, and instantaneous architectural project

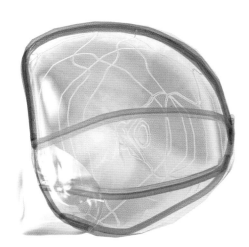

state O

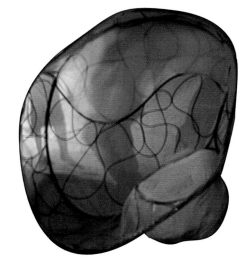

state I

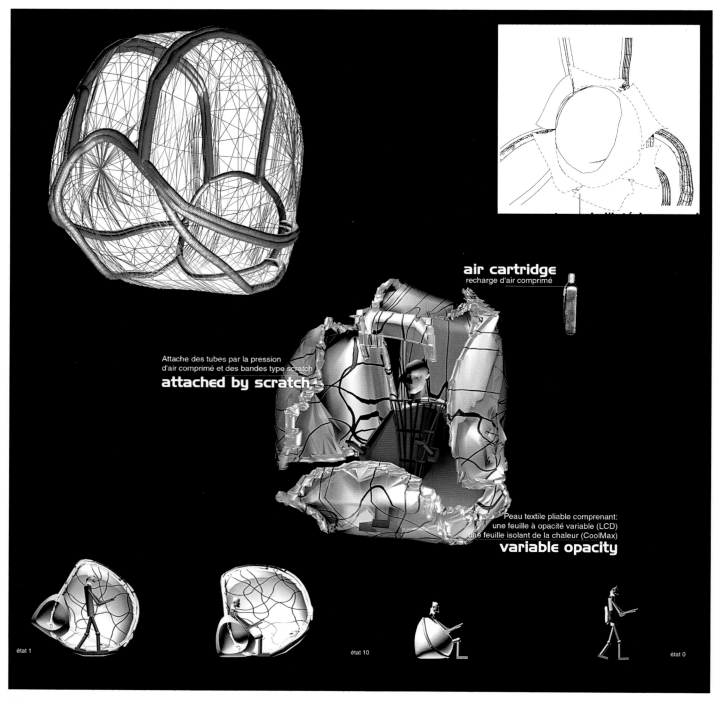

air cartridge
recharge d'air comprimé

Attache des tubes par la pression
d'air comprimé et des bandes type scratch
attached by scratch

Peau textile pliable comprenant:
une feuille à opacité variable (LCD)
une feuille isolant de la chaleur (CoolMax)
variable opacity

état 1

état 10

état 0

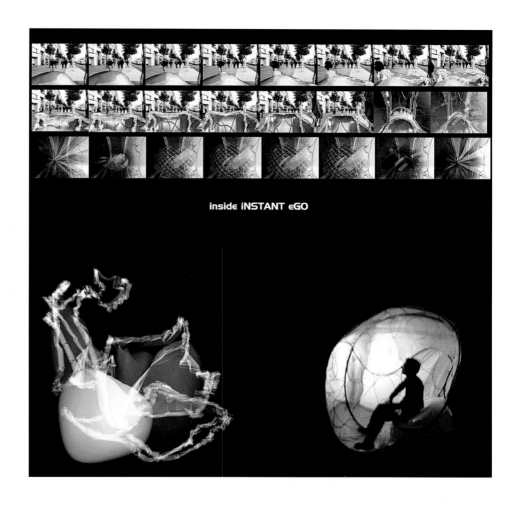

inside iNSTANT eGO

Reason

Engaging into the speeds of a future, imagined metropolis the association Pod supplies a set of "machines" deployed vis-à-vis the city. Bypassing the conventional unity of architectural representation, (*i.e.*: the building), Po.D constructs a new relationship between experiences of the public and private through a collapsible membrane that stands at the point of inflexion between the two. The project "iNSTANT eGO" consists of a shield, to be used at will by the individual within an urbanity presumed hostile. It is, in actuality an instrument by which one could regress into an infantile, dream-like world, a collective con-sensual hallucination. Or vanish from the face of the city – on a line of flight "iNSTANT eGO" also represents a growing tendency on the part of Young Architects world over. A new irruption exploring a nascent "I" and its indulgences, or a situation where architecture is used, again, as an art of illusion, a 'lens' that shapes the external world by shaping itself. Po.D as an organisation well represents the characterisation of a new Europe as set by the "Aims and Finalities" of the Borromini Award. Ideas and institutions of European extraction have spawned an association spanning three continents and with a dozen languages – a vast domain exemplifying "a geographical and cultural space whose borders remain", as they must, "undefined" – a nomad space which is inherently problematic. *Anand Bhatt*

S&Aa

Federico Soriano
(Spain, 61)
Dolores Palacios
(Spain, 60)

EUSKALDUNA JAUREGIA
Congress and Music Centre

Dimensions: 45.000 sq.m
Client: Bizkaiko Foru Aldundia
Place of construction: Bilbao, Spain
Date of completion: 1998

S&Aa Federico Soriano Architect graduated from
E.T.S.A.M. in 1986. Associate Professor of Design at
the Escuela Técnica Superior de Arquitectura de Madrid.
(E.T.S.A.M.) Director-Editor of the journal Fisuras de la
Cultura Contemporánea.
Dolores Palacios Architect graduated from E.T.S.A.M.
in 1986. Associate Professor of Design at Alfonso X El
Sabio University (Madrid). Writer for the journal ViA.

The image of the Bilbao estuary is one of activity and building. Consequently our project must bear in mind a form that is constantly changing, or at least a form that is frozen at one moment in its formation. An object that would seem to be permanently under construction. The Palacio Euskalduna rises like the gigantic remains of a ship, a ghost ship, that should have been built a long time ago in the old Astilleros Euskalduna boatyards but was abandoned and left to sink into the muddy depths of the estuary. Its shape and construction recall the shape of a ship. Its shape and rivets seem to have rusted. All we shall do is to clean up the interior and place within it, as in the holds of a ship, the various theatres and the great spaces that its use as an opera house demands. Having propped it up in a dry dock, as is only proper, we shall transform this rusty shell into a musical box.

The double skin of its interior will provide insulation and the most appropriate acoustic form for each of the three halls or theatres. In each empty hold we shall support or hang plates, platforms, nets, of wood or wire mesh. Some will serve as tiered seating, others will be acoustic ceilings. The rest of the empty ship will hold workshops, stages and store rooms in its great interior space. We shall simply attach some towers, like scaffolding, to accommodate the dressing rooms, the lobbies and restaurants, the offices, etc. The brief demands a double use, if not simultaneously certainly almost continuously as an opera house and a conference centre. We

shall therefore build two interwoven lobbies, made one by their shared empty spaces, with their platforms abutted at different levels (one for opera and one for congresses), in order to provide separate accesses to the auditoriums. Each platform will only serve one of the two uses and will have its own entrances and exits. In this way in extreme cases, the main auditorium could be emptying by one set of doors and foyers while people are entering by other doors and foyers, without the two sets of circulation ever meeting, while the metal wall of the auditorium would dominate the empty spaces.

The building, so constituted, has no scale. Its significant form is structured with reference to its own rules. It has no shape, as it is the result of building a dense, compact section that will contain all the required uses (halves of theatres, storage spaces, workshops, stage gridirons) within itself. Neither do we impose details on it. The volume of the shoulders juts out at the precise moment when this becomes necessary. The building has lost its edges. They make their appearance like walled limits that mark off the interior supporting space. However, the form that will be recognisable will never be these, only that of the ship. And this is in the modern manner, with the space inside the wall empty and usable. Lastly, it is a building we wish to be recognised as without gestures. In a way, we would like it to be something impersonal, as its origin is more dependant on other laws than on those that our taste might autonomously dictate.

General view

Reason

One of the most
interesting features of
Federico Soriano and
Dolores Palacios as a
team of architecture is
their sense of the project,
rigorous and playful
at the same time.
That is to say, their
projects seem to have
been conceived in an
enjoying way, but the
truth is that there is a
deep discipline behind
them.
Another reason why I
recommend them, and
one can notice it clearly
as looking at the
Euskalduna Jauregia, is
the relation with the site,
which is not imitative but
interactive. What they do
from the site is catching
the unexpected – and
hidden – potentials and
stimulating the singular
situations. They use
these words to explain
this attribute, referring
to the opera house and
conference centre: "The
building, so constituted,
has no scale. Its
significant form is
structured with reference
to its own rules. [...] Its
origin is more dependant
on other laws than on
those that our taste might
autonomously dictate."
Finally, I would point
up their bet for the
imagination and their
capacity for the surprise;
their plastic will and
their strategic attitude.
As I said at the beginning,
they own this valuable
ability to combine play
and rigor.
Manuel Gausa

Sadar Vuga Arhitekti

Jurij Sadar
(Slovenia, 1963)
Boštjan Vuga
(Slovenia, 1966)

The Chamber Of Commerce And Industry Office Building

Dimensions: 4640 sq.m
Client: Chamber of Commerce and Industry of Slovenia
Place of construction: Lubljana, Slovenia
Date of completion: 1999

Office profile
Name: Sadar Vuga Arhitekti, d.o.o.
company registered: October 23rd, 1996

Primary activity
architectural design, landscape design, civil engineering and related technical consulting, regional planning and urban planning.

Founders and proprietors
Jurij Sadar, 50% capital share, Bo?tjan Vuga, 50% capital share.

Professional members details
Sadar Vuga Arhitekti company is licensed at the Slovenian Chamber of Engineers (IZS 0009). Sadar Vuga Arhitekti is a member of the international network of architectural practices O.C.E.A.N. net.

Working method
we feel that integrative designing is the essence of our architectural production. We do not believe in the superiority of the individual mind. That is the only way to design effective unconventional products. Each of our architectural products stands on its own, for it arises from different spatial situations, investors' desires, investment outlay and other external causes.
We create today for tomorrow. Our sense of today's era does not mould us into currently prominent trends of architectural production. We wish to transcend them. We dare to anticipate tendencies that can generate new architectural effects.

The new building for the Chamber of Commerce and Industry of Slovenia (CCIS) represents a step forward from the industrial towards the computerized and displays new relationships which are no longer based on a goods/price relationship, but on the ability to adapt to the rising and varying needs of the market. Globalisation of the economy in the era of late capitalism, by the disappearance of physical borders, affect the new formulation of urban topographies. The complex systems of non-hierarchical structure will enable fast movement and dislocation of the program's character. CCIS is a megastore of capital and the generator of economic development of the region. The corporate design reflecting such a profile, and at the same time also the ambiguity of function, has been carried out thoroughly: from the basic composition of volume to the elements of visual identity.

Sadar Vuga Arhitekti think through diagrams. The already mentioned ambiguity of CCIS function, related to the official and semi-public part, usually treated by public *breitfuss* and internal superstructure, is interpreted here in a new, more active way by raising the basis into the vertical and resulting in numerous possible interactions and new spatial and functional variations in the use of business premises.

The second important diagram shows the possible flows, as a consequence of the mentioned transformation and permeation of the external and internal space. The engaged logistic of use and spatial mathematics will result, maybe for the authors themselves as well, in surprisingly efficient versions of exploitation.

The square in front of the house is the third part of the diagram and represents a response to the urban position of the house in Dimieva Road. It is not the "rest of the plot", but a space with its own operative logic of limited public usage. Considering the already expressed high interest of the public for the promotional and representative events in the external space of CCIS, it is not hard to imagine a whole series of possible scenarios. Even in this segment, Sadar Vuga Arhitekti reach out for the ready-made instruments – here, in fact, borrowed from the range of horizontal traffic signalling, in combination with rubber and with floor illumination, thus underlining the integrity of *plaza* and its emptied condition.

Designing the interior and the graphical identity of CCIS, provide a positive counterbalance to the basic design process of the house. The choice of national furniture further underlines the image of a "Slovenian house"… with its soft lines and echoes of the seventies, it adjusts well to the geometrical precision of the vertical hall.

(Source: ORIS 3, "Magazine for Architecture and culture" III-3-99, Hrvoje Njiri).

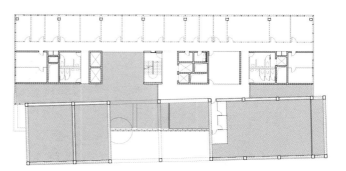

The side front

Longitudinal and
transversal section

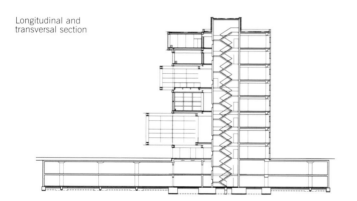
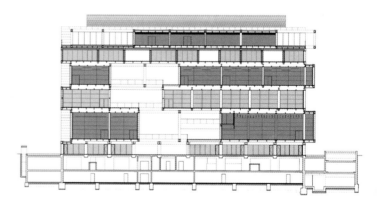

Reason

This project, partly a conversion, partly an extension, combines the existing and the new architecture in an incredibly convincing way in a new whole. The modern appearance is a symbol for the desire to link up with global networks, the fractured appearance for the desire for democracy and the general concept, treating the building as a "megastore" with a low threshold for people that want to start their own business. Thereby it makes the organization really work like a client-friendly organisation, a store where people can shop for advice, information, training and services instead of a bureaucratic institution. Apart from that the building is carefully detailed and offers a beautiful transparent and open spatiality.
Bart Lootsma

Zoe Samourkas
(Greece, 1962)

Apartment in Palaio Psychico

Dimensions: approx. 440 sq.m
Client: family of the architect
Place of construction: Athens, Greece
Date of completion: 2000

Year degree received: 1989
Degree: Degree in Architecture
Name of school: National Technical University
Location of school: Athens, Greece
Since 1993 in practice in Athens

Major competitions
Battle of Crete 1941, Memorial, Museum and
Conference Center, Galatas-Chania, Crete, 1991.

Major works completed
Athens Tower's 18th floor offices-Reconstruction, Athens,
Greece, 1995.
Apartment in Philothei, Athens, Greece, 1999.
Apartment in Palaio Psychico, Athens, Greece, 2000.

Located in a transitional zone, between the urban center of the city and the outer suburbs, the house is situated in a small site facing a park. It is a house for a family who needed spacious reception areas for social occasions. It is structured on three levels: entrance, garage and service areas on the ground floor, living and dining spaces on the first and bedrooms on the second.

The building evolves the plans, sections and elevations through a single idea of intersections. All levels are separated from each other creating horizontal empty spaces between them. This gives a sense of lightness from the exterior of the building and beautiful views to the park from the interior. It also emphasizes the asymmetrical arrangement of the open air 'rooms' and lets the air circulate through the building. In the entrance one meets a "petrify" garden from concrete while the traditional garden of the house could said to be found in the park opposite.

The circulation is linear and parallel to the central concrete wall while a long and narrow skylight on the roof of the second floor diffuses the natural light along it. Furthermore, all vertical circulation and services hinge on the central structural spine.

With the exception of the openings leading to the four open-air "rooms", the long elevations of the building are protected from the sun and are given privacy by a zone of horizontal wooden slats which at the same time defines the scale of these elevations. Exposed concrete is used throughout the building. All the materials are used in their natural condition and every constructional detail follows the general principles of the simplicity of the design, since all elements are integral parts of its entity.

Outside details

Inside detail

Reason

The house, located in a suburb of Athens facing a small park and structured on three levels, is worked out in plan, section and elevation through a single idea: "All levels are separated from each other creating empty spaces between them. This gives a sense of lightness and also emphasises the anti-symmetrical arrangement of the open air rooms." The circulation is linear, parallel to the longitudinal axis of the building; all vertical circulation and services revolve around the central structural spine. The entire building is made out of exposed concrete, accentuating its monolithic structure. With the exception of the openings to the four open-air "rooms", the long elevations of the building are protected by a zone of wooden horizontal blinds which at the same time resolve the scale of the elevations. Without doubts, the emphasis in this project is put in the tectonics of the building – with an attention for well designed and well executed detailing. In reference to a trendy ephemeral or even formless stream of contemporary architecture it re-establishes a continuity with the neglected perfection of modernism within the "conservative" realm of the private house. *Yorgos Simeoforodis*

Stéphane Schurdi-Levraud
(France, 1967)

Maison Combes

Dimensions: 179 sq.m
Client: Mr. & Mrs. Combes
Place of construction: Léognan, Bordeaux, France
Date of completion: 1998

He graduated at the Bordeaux School of Architecture on 12 June 1997. He began working as a freelance architect in Bordeaux on 1 October 1997.
He established a studio of architects on 1 May 1998.
He registered with the Regional Register of Architects with general number 43352 and regional number 1516 on 27 October 1998.

Experience in the private sector
Combes Home in Léognan,1997-1998.
House in Corsica, competition, project completed in March 1999.
Industrial building for the IT sector, 2000.
Vivien Home in Beychac (33), 1999-2000.

Experience in the public sector
Restructure and expansion of a kindergarten/nursery in a department store in Bordeaux.
Renovation of "Piazza della Vittoria" in Bordeaux.
Creation of a warehouse in Dax (Landes).

Student competitions
Butagaz Competition, Signs of survival/1994/ "Being on a road without signs is like being Alain Colas without indications: you lose touch and then submerge", Paris.
Competition for the French Centre of Electricity and Architecture /1994/ "Design and create a town hall", 3rd prize, M. Fuksas, special award from the jury.
UIA Competition in Barcelona/1996/ "Homes and public spaces in the centre of Barcelona", Spain.
Competition for the French Centre of Electricity and Architecture /1996/ "Design and create an EDF-GDF agency", C. Hauvettes, award from the jury.

Degree Theses
"6540 sq.m in the centre of town", restructuring of homes in the St Jean Tower, 12 June 1997, Bordeaux. J. Hondelatte, award from the jury.

Overview: this project was designed for Mr. and Mrs. Combes, who are sixty-year old bakers, in a village called Léognan, near Bordeaux. The initial idea was for a 180 sq.m house located on 3180 sq.m of land. The piece of land was located in Rue de Granjean – north of Léognan. There was already a very run-down building on the land in question, which was to be demolished. The land is surrounded by a 2 meter-high wall in cement slabs and there is only one entrance – from Granjean Road. The land slopes slightly and is covered in short vegetation and a few badly-kept copses and a lime tree. There is also a 50 meter-deep ground water table.
Project: first of all, there is a building. The material enwraps the shape and silhouette of what could be a simple pavilion. Just one material, always the same material, just one creation, zinc mesh covers the entire house. There is no roof, no facade – it is a kind of packaging.
The shape is almost brutal (two-pitch roof, 30% protuberance, visible pinions), a minimum expression of the need to host something and a reply – without derogation – to the P.O.S. town planning scheme.
The violence of this habitat - which would be simplified or purified – therefore disappears. On approaching, you realize that it is not just a simplification or an abstraction. The technical aspect to the finishing details, the way the materials have been used, the systems adopted to open and hide spaces, creates and gives life to something complex. The way the house has been mechanized demonstrates the need to enrich and improve the livable space (the quality given to spaces). The huge windows can be used to open the space in which one lives to the outdoors. The lines of the windows are mortised to ensure continuity with the outdoor land. The motorized and remote-controlled roller shutters leave the freedom to close the entire house when

desired. The internal flooring, heating system (in the floor) and insulation are of a good quality.
The comfort and domestic character of the house are also provided through the profitability of the constructed livable surface. The room layout proposed by the customer was rather classic: living room, kitchen, studio, bathroom, etc. However, the request for a guestroom and winter garden made the overall requirements particular. These two areas are enclosed by sliding windows and mobile walls and are located in the heart of the house. The way they are used ensures a kind of absence of space for circulation (corridor, storeroom), to increase the surface area and produce an unseparated volume – some of which are located between the rooms (see rural habitat, only livable room). Each area is taken the most possible advantage of as it is used for a purpose.
In order to free the livable area, the more important areas have been grouped together (kitchen, toilet, storeroom, etc.). As we did not wish to radicalize everything through optimization, the rather bulky furniture of Mr. and Mrs. Combes was taken into account. Areas to include the large country-style furniture were reserved in the new house.
Various materials were used in the structure. The metal parts involve steel beams and a brick wall. This was chosen as a compromise between the purely constructive wish to use a single structural principle (metal) and the legitimate request to use brickwork from the customer.
The overall cost was 980,000 French Francs for 170 sq.m, i.e. 5,500 French Francs per square meter. The project could have cost less, however it could also have cost more. The project was not implemented using the minimum cost possible, but the initial budget.
(Combes House, Léognan, Gironda, 1997/1998 – in collaboration with Oriane Deville).

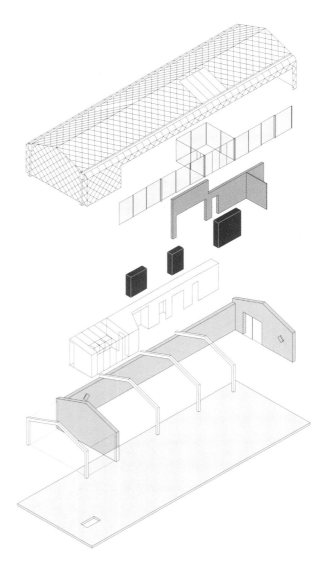

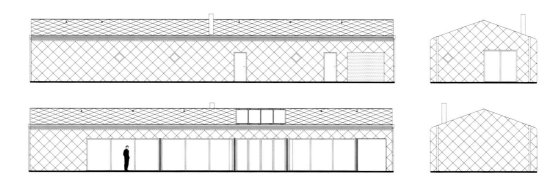

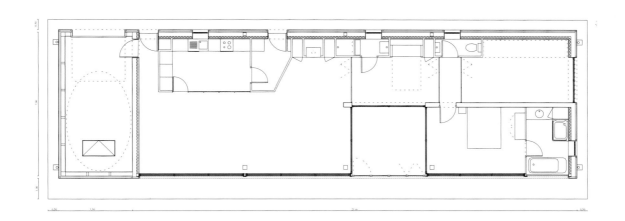

Reason

This is an ordinary/extraordinary project: the first work by a thirty-year-old architect. One would not expect the clients to be inclined towards adventure (a couple of bakers in their sixties, very much devoted to a certain type of architecture and to a certain concept of "home"). Add to this an unpredictable site condition consisting of bare ground covered by lifeless vegetation surrounded by a two-meter-high concrete slab

wall, where the water table is just below the surface. Initially it seemed that nothing would go well. And yet, things gradually started to work out, thanks to a patient mutual listening process. The result was an almost ordinary, almost normal, almost banal project, whose peculiarity, though, stems just from the subtle shading of meaning in the different uses of the term "almost". From the outside, the house appearance reminds one of an elongated Monopoly

house, stretched on the ground with four square walls and a symmetrical roof. Everything is sheathed with a reptilian-looking "skin" of zinc diamond-shaped plates, which makes the house look like a precious leather item. This skin wraps the volume, like gift wrapping, with accurately folded corners. The minimal definition of the walls and the roof are an emblematic sign of the prototypical house which calls into question the inconsequential small houses scattered around the area like metastases.

Inside, the plan does not follow the sequence of delineated spaces standard to a house: entrance, corridor, living room, dining room, bedroom, bathroom. It consists instead of open zones of space overlayed between the four perimeter walls. Interior walls are located only where and when they are absolutely necessary, and then they are preferably movable and transparent. A "mechanical" path runs along one of the elevations, lining up the main "wet" functions (cooking, washing,

heating, etc.) The rest is organized more or less depending on specific circumstances, which are exempt from the standardized regularity of day-to-day activities. There is also room for the clients' personal effects, which adds some spice to the overall effect. The clients like their furniture which consists of a strange unnatural hybrid between unsold stock from the Salvation Army and the first illegal exports that were "Made in Hong Kong" from the post-war years. It doesn't matter, the plan follows their

shape, folding in and out to provide niches where these objects will be on display, as if floating in an axonometric projection. There are several features of this house which will give the clients the impression of living in a "normal house", the incorporation of the client's furniture into the scheme and the incorporation of a single brick wall into the steel structure. In the end, everyone is happy...
Yves Nacher

Studio dd1479

Daniela Moderini
(Italy, 1963)
Laura Zampieri
(Italy, 1963)

Hanging gardens, Venezia

Dimensions: 400 sq.m
Client: Hans Wagner, Wire Technology
Place of construction: Venice, Italy
Date of construction: 1999

Daniela Moderini graduated from the School of Architecture at Venice University in 1990. Since 1998 she has been a professor under contract with the architecture faculty in Ferrara. Laura Zampieri was born in San Vito al Tagliamento in 1963. In 1992, she graduated from the School of Architecture at Venice University, where she performs research and contributes to university teaching.
The two architects' professional activity is complemented by research and university teaching, with particular emphasis on urban design and landscaping. Since 1995 they have worked towards developing the new urban planning scheme for Venice. Their commissions include landscape and architectural projects for private clients. They have taken part in numerous competitions in Italy and abroad.

The design of the hanging gardens is part of a broad programme to rebuild a portion of the former distillery building, a monument of industrial archaeology, located in the Giudecca near the Stucky mill.
The design of the interior space by architects Michael Carapetian and Raul Pantaleo consists of developing a habitation that has its fulcrum in the room dedicated to music. The intervention on the exterior extends over two large terraces open to the *bora* and *scirocco* winds.
The two hanging gardens, conceived as an extension of the interior space to the north towards Venice and to the south towards the lagoon – whose pedestrian elevation they maintain – are different places, united by the strong, characterizing presence of bamboo.
A series of steel I-beams, raised to reach the required elevation and not bearing on the existing floor, support stainless steel frames and teak or stone staves; the water basins and the flower boxes are hung on the structure and disappear under the level of the pavement.
The north terrace, the location of representation and entry to the project, is designed like the deck of a ship out of which rise the bamboo elements, of different heights and colour. It is a flexible space that may be adapted to *collective* uses and more everyday uses, and modified by moving the large, wheeled plant containers. The south terrace, facing the lagoon, is a more private place. A strip of water, in slight movement, divides the space, and a raised dais, immersed in the creeping rosemary, directs the eye over the boundary wall, towards the exterior.

Garden floor and detail

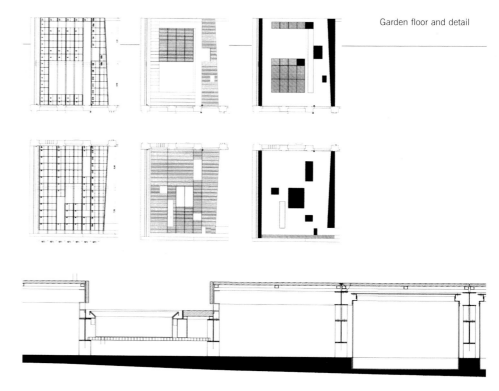

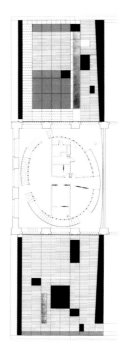

Main floor

General view, path and plantation details

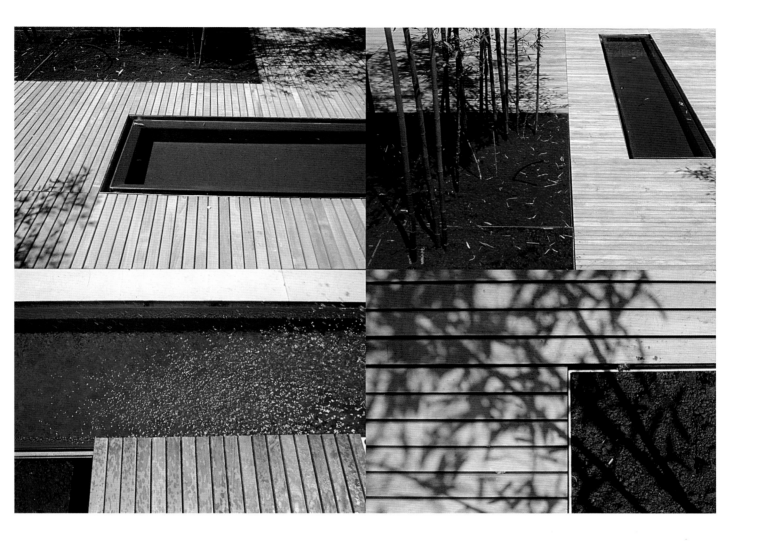

Reason

While this project is ephemeral and poetic, it is also precise and concrete. The landscape "demarche" seems to be one of the emerging features in the generation of young architects, the result of an "ecological" awareness, in relation to both the natural and the man-made environments. This project is part of the restoration plan of a former distillery. The project creates a meditative space which opens itself towards a complex city, which is rarely perceived from above. The meticulous design of the surface and the refined technical details (raised steel I-beams, stainless steel frames, teak and stone staves, rolling plant containers) manage to break down and enhance the different parts of the "surface" that is intended for both collective and private use.

The project's quality is expressed through simplicity and technical details. The concept itself of a "roof garden" refers to the specific characteristics of the surrounding city, to the representation of its landscape, as well as its technical aspects.
Yorgos Simeoforodis

Studio R&Sie.D/B:L

François Roche
(France, 1961)

Blur Style – Indistinct Style
in the City as in the Country

Dimensions: 3 sq.m and 5000 sq.m
Client: Caisse des Dépots and Consignation Section
mécénat, Paris
Place of construction: Paris et la Baîse
Date of completion: 1997-1998

Exhibition by 40 architects under 40 years old at
the French Institute of Architecture in 1990.
Exposition Action, projects from 1987 to 1993 at
the French Institute of Architecture in March and April
1993.
Villa Medici Award outside the walls, 1994; selected for
the Architectural Exhibit in Venice in 1991, in 1996 in
the French pavilion, in 2000 in the French pavilion and
in the International one.
Trans-Architecture June 3, 1998 in Berlin, Rotterdam.
Mutations @morphes, Orléans, Los Angeles, New-York
from September 1998 to February 2000.
Archilab, Orléans, session 1999.
Professor at ENSBA since 1999.
Professor at the Bartlett School (unit 22) in London
for 2000-2001.

Studio-Competition-Projects (selection)
La Defense, 2000/2001, Unplug Tower.
Shinano (Japan), 2000/2001, "Fish-breeding" Complex
and Restaurant.
Houston, Malmoe, Nasa, 1999/2000, Earth Unit,
Future Homes.
Montpellier, 1999/2000, Individual Home.
Pouilly, 1999, Bridge Restaurant, 1999.
Rotterdam, Town-planning 1999, commissioned by NAI.
Johannesburg, Soweto, 1997, the Museum Memorial.
Venezia, School of Architecture, 1998.
Vianne, la Baîse, 1996, a fluvial arrangement.
La Reunion, the Villa Medici of the Indian Ocean, 1997.
Sarcelles, 30 experimental homes.
Paris, the Deligny Pool.
San Francisco, the re-arrangement of the Bay along
7 km of coastline.
Montréal, Place d'Youville, urban planning.
Berlin, the Parliament on the Sprea.
Paris, Japanese Cultural Home.
Trébeurden, a building on the ocean front,
infrastructures.

Exhibits
Venice,Biennal, French and International Pavilion,
June-September 2000.
Los Angeles, "An Oblique Lineage Toward Hypersurface",
L.Stern Gallery, April 2000.
New-York, Mutations @morphes 3.0, Columbia,
February-March 2000.
Paris, Purple Institute, e-space/genesis,
December 10-13 1999.
Los Angeles, UCLA, Mutations @morphes 3.0,
November-December 1999.
Monaco, "Desire", September-November 1999.
Orleans, Archi-Lab, April-May 1999.
Rotterdam, Nai, Urban-planning project,
April-June 1999.

The work of our office, R&Sie.D/B:L seeks to connect architecture to a distortion of cartography and
to geography. Localism thus becomes the support
for a mutation, produced on the physical existence
of a territory. It is about "hyperlocalism", a long way
from the meanings attributed to an attitude of
macrostructure, but something existing "Right
Here, Right Now", to make reference to the song
by Fat Boy Slim.
   This involvement with immediacy, the si-
multaneity of perception, allows us to escape any projected influence or suggestion, mental or metaphorical, of the global system. The whole functions as a
link with microstructure, whose implication and involvement derive from an analysis of each situation.

These two projects, realized for the same
client, act on an indistinct logic. In this way, via the
process of distortion, the nature of the mutations is
made clear.
   Our projects infiltrate and impress themselves
upon the things they were able to transform, like
the now famous computer virus "I Love You". The
world is a blur, between the virtual and the real,
between Terminator, The Matrix and my grand-
mother/housekeeper. It is like imagining that what
is visible here, becomes invisible elsewhere. The de-
formation caused by transplantation, is a result of
genetics, the antithesis of the *tabula rasa*, and the
decoration of domestic wallpaper, thus creating a
third way, a hybrid…

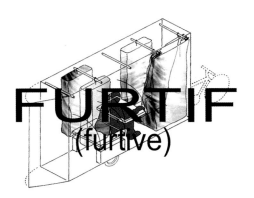

The park and the
happening

Reasons

Since these two projects do not belong to the "building" category, one might wonder whether their presence at this Prize is legitimate. However, the relationship with the surrounding territory, with respect to the way they fit into it, and their endless search for answers, represent a work as legitimate as anyone consisting of a so-called lasting building. Indeed, their strength is mainly related to the transition space they find their way into. A transition space or, rather, a fluctuating area, rarely used by architects. These two projects are absolutely consistent with each other, and form a perfect whole. They represent the contemporary condition of the city-rat on one hand, and of the field-mouse on the other. But, unlike in La Fontaine's fairy tales, we are not here to judge, but are simply part of the world of possibility: the blurred reality of our contemporary society. This is the reason why this dual project (outside the built environment? In its conventional meaning?) deserves all our consideration.
Didier Fiuza Faustino

Roche DSV & Sie.P have a work trajectory characterised by a new "contact with nature", more literal at the beginning and more manipulated and sophisticated in their last projects. It's a kind of combination between mimesis and recycling. They pay much attention to the site, to the context, to the local features, trying to analyse them from a synthetic, abstract and understanding dimension; trying to stimulate the force vectors of the local and their hidden requests. They call this interest for the local "hyperlocalism". Another attribute to notice is the re-invention they make of the form by manipulating any virtual or physical information. As they say, "the world is blur, between 'virtuality' and reality". Lastly, I would emphasize that, during the process of the project, they play with the geographic more than with the volumetric. They say it in their presentation: "we try to connect architecture to a distortion of the cartography, the geography".
Manuel Gausa

Kerstin Thompson
(Australia, 1965)

West Coast House

Dimensions: 180 sq.m
Client: not disclosed
Place of construction: Skenes Creek, Victoria, Australia
Date of completion: 1999

Current PositionsPrincipal of Kerstin Thompson
Architects Pty Ltd.

Architectural & Urban Design projects
1998, completed Masters of Architecture at RMIT.
1994, established Kerstin Thompson Architects P/L.
1994-1990, lecturer in Design at Dept. Architecture,
RMIT.
1990, worked with Perrott Lyon Mathieson Pty Ltd as
Assistant Site Architect on the Telecom Corporate Tower.
Part time Sole practitioner
1987-1986, Architectural, Industrial and Furniture
Design in the Milan Studio of Matteo Thun; worked
with MMH Partnership. Work included the design
& documentation of commercial projects.

Selected Awards
1999, Seppelt Contemporary Art Award for
Environmental Design.
Shortlisted for National RAIA Award for Residential
architecture.
1999, RAIA Harold Desbrowe-Annear Award for Apollo
Bay House, Victoria.
1999, RAIA Merit Award for James Service Place,
South Melbourne.
1996, RAIA Merit Award for Webb Street Fitzroy.
1993, CHASA Refereed Design Award for Lorne House.

Selected Projects – Current
RMIT Technology Estate – LLLF Building and
Masterplan. Stage 1, 3500 sq.m; stage 1-5, 17.500
sq.m approx.
Multiple Residential development to Webb Street, Fitzroy.
3000 sq.m approx.
Fitzroy warehouse redevelopment. Approx. 855m².
Fit out to Medweb office in St Kilda Road, Melbourne.
New residence to Paringa Road Portsea.
New residence and Landscape Masterplan at Lake
Connawarre.
New residence and Landscape Masterplan, Benwerrin,
Victoria.

Project description: on the top of a rural site with
extensive views across Bass Strait and the Otways,
this house responds to various idiosyncrasies of the
site and is comprised of two primary gestures: a concrete block wall which rises up from the ground loop-
ing to form interior and exterior living spaces and,
nestled alongside this, a cedar box containing bedrooms, bathrooms and the kitchen.

*Relationship of the Project ti its Site and Con-
text:* the form was determined in part by the vicis-
situdes of the site: the plan winds its way around
three significant gum trees; the floor levels of the
dwelling reflect the changing site levels minimising
the extent of excavation required and lessening ad-
verse impact of the building on the existing ecol-
ogy; and the main elements form a wall to establish sheltered areas protected from the south-east
and north west winds characteristic of the site. The
position and form of openings were designed for specific views and reading of the landscape; some focus on the ground and others to the distant sea or
mountain views. The materials were chosen to res-
onate with the existing landscape; for example the
cedar cladding echoes the verticality of the surrounding gum trees, and the concrete blocks em-
phasise the horizontal expanse of the site.

Cost effectivness: standard construction
techniques were used throughout to minimise cost.
Finishes were kept simple and cost effective. Materials such as Armourply flooring were selected
for their cost effectiveness and exploited for their
design appropriateness to a robust and unfussy
building.

Costings were undertaken at Schematic Design and Design Development to monitor the com-
patibility of the client's wishes with the budget. The
tender price was an accurate reflection of the Design Development costing. A 3% increase on the
contract price was recorded at the end of construction.

Structure, Construction, Materials, Services:
the building exploits the design opportunities of standard construction techniques throughout for cost effectiveness and architectural interest. The two construction types were masonry using concrete block,
and timber framing with a light weight timber
cladding. These were complimentary to the development of the bi-polar design strategy.

The collected runoff from the expansive roof
is stored in the onsite water tanks. The clients were
committed to using hydronic heating and gas cook-
ware powered by LPG gas.

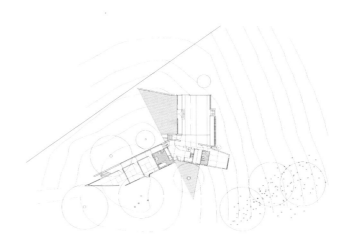

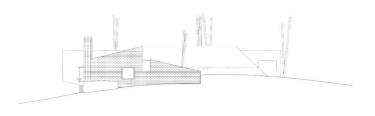

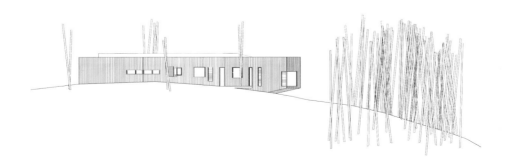

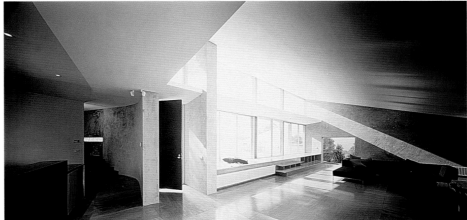

Reason

The work of Kerstin Thompson, particularly in the West Coast House, Apollo Bay, Victoria, Australia, provides a clear program of family life and growth. Here is the extension of the hanging moments of lazy afternoons into a lifetime of potential development but also the attempt to seek a new way of relating to the new land, the Australian landscape, to find cultural meaning in nature.
Houses by architects are in tension between the history of the villa and the specific experience of the site and client, but here a near perfect balance between the ambitions of architectural form and a rich choreography of family living has been found.
Ross Jenner

vehovar&jauslin Architektur

Mateja Vehovar
(Slovenia, 1961)
Stefan Jauslin
(Switzerland, 1968)

Mateja Vehovar and Stefan Jauslin founded vehovar & jauslin Architektur in 1997 in Zurich. The studio operates in the fields of architecture, landscape architecture, public space, exhibition design, urban planning, and media installations.
In their work, Vehovar and Jauslin seek to cross boundaries. The integration of disciplines beyond the traditional field of building industry is very important to them.
Their recent work includes: several housing projects, an ephemeral exhibition building for the Swiss National Exhibition, an interactive exhibition on artificial intelligence, an interactive light installation in a public square, and the new Christmas lighting for the city of Zug.
Vehovar and Jauslin have received numerous prizes in prestigious competitions. In 1999 they were awarded the Swiss Federal Award for the Arts.

Renovation of a stairway and an office, Wohlen

Dimensions: 1100 sq.m
Client: Victory org
Place of construction: Wohlen, Switzerland
Date of completion: 1998

The existing industrial building complex of the 70ies and 80ies is located in the vicinity of Zurich. The prefabricated structure is visible, both inside and outside. The project concerns an office space and the staircase, the main connection between the three floors. The new intervention exposes the modular structure and openness of the space as originally conceived. The installations are of a temporary character, they facilitate future change if required. The office is converted into an open plan of connected zones, open to a uniform ceiling. Individual working places contain simultaneously the atmosphere of privacy, as well as an openness to the whole. Different program requirements overlap.

Each zone simultaneously fulfils different functions. Adaptable shelves create an internal zoning. The back of the shelving units is covered with back-lit fiberglass. The shelves are thus dematerialized to glowing elements. The circulation area as an area of staging is treated as a place where "spectators" and "actors" meet. Consequently two open and transparent stairs are newly introduced. The views can flow in many directions so that the space can be overlooked in its total extension. A bluish fiberglass screen represents on one hand an inner separation between vertical and horizontal movement, on the other hand people are still recognizable through it by their shape. This screen tints the daylight in a surreal way.

The main stair and the office space

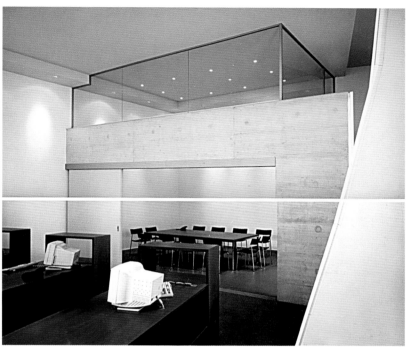

Reason

Mateja Vehovar and Stefan Jauslin (V.&J.) founded vehovar & jauslin Architektur in 1997 in Zurich. Their studio engages in the fields of architecture, landscape architecture, public space and exhibition design, urban planning, and media installations. In their work V.&J. transcend boundaries to seek the integration of disciplines outside the traditional field of building industry. Among their recent works are not only housing and school projects, but also an interactive light installation on a public square, the new Christmas lighting for the city of Zug, an interactive exhibition on artificial intelligence and an ephemeral exhibition building for the Swiss national exhibition Expo.02 in 2002. The very ambitious Expo.02 exhibition will be simultaneously located on the shores of three lakes and in four towns; millions of visitors are expected. V.&J. won the competition for the architectural structure of the site at Yverdon-les-Bains. The structure will host various exhibitions with different themes which will determine the architectonic language as well as the surrounding landscape design. A sensual dimension to the site will be contributed by rolling artificial hills, the aphrodisiac perfumes of plants, multimedia installations and suggestive sounds. For this project V.&J. invited Tristan Kobler, Elizabeth Diller and Ricardo Scofidio and Adriaan Geuze from West 8 to collaborate with them, founding the group »extasia".
With their embracing affinity to artists and passionate devotion to interdisciplinary and experimental research, V.&J. are architects with significant promise.
Jacqueline Burckhardt

Choi Wook
(Korea, 1963)

Ilsan studio for sculptor

Dimensions: 330 sq.m
Client: a sculptor
Place of construction: Ilsan, kyung-gi-do, Korea
Date of completion: 1999

Choi Wook received his BA degree in Architecture from the Hong Ik University in Korea in 1985 and a Doctorate in Architecture from the School of Architecture at Venice University, Venice, Italy in 1989. He was awarded a Macdowell Colony Fellowship in the USA in 1998.
He established K&C Associates in 1992 and Studio Choiwook in 2000. He has also been an instructor at the Korean National University of Arts, Department of Architecture School of Visual Arts since 1999.

When I was commissioned to design the Ilsan studio for a sculptor, I was asked to design a space for research and making study models and not for making the actual sculptures. The site is located on the outskirts of a city; there is a hill full of trees; in front a continuous space form outside to inside. I instantly thought of making the interior and exterior as one continuous and fluid space by designing glass walls on both front and back of the building. In addition, the interior space has no shadows since the light is coming in from three different directions. As result, the interior space naturally feels more exterior.

Main views

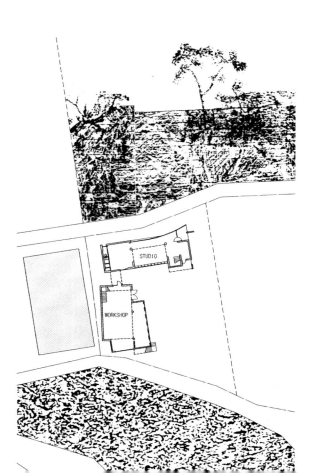

The entrance, the passage
and the workshop

The main facades

Reason

Wook Choi is part of the new generation of Korean architects. Unlike his colleagues who mainly studied in the US (or sometimes in France), he chose Venice, Italy, to widen his academic and cultural panorama. This unusual (in the Korean context) experience has certainly left prints in his practice although not in an ostentatious manner. With the N weekend house, Choi shows his skills to marry a contemporary reflection with a nonetheless classical attitude (in the good meaning of terms). No utopian conception of the domestic space and practices, nor the use of an "avant-garde" architectural language. The horizontality of the project, the division of space and the game with solid and hollow parts of the building are as much references to the Korean vernacular house. Nevertheless, this intelligent integration of cultural heritage, the elegant lines of the construction, the sound balance of light and darkness are definitely of our time. Far from a yin/yang conception and interpretation that most western architects are always eager to do, the N Weekend House is a subtle and clever reflection on the contrast between our almost immutable needs (sleep, eat...) and our permanent desire of difference. And when you look at it, it stands still as an evident answer to the chaotic world within which it lives.
Didier Fiuza Faustino

Zoo Architects

Peter Richardson
(UK, 1962)
Robin Lee
(UK, 1966)
Vivien Mason
(UK, 1971)

Zoo was founded in 1996 by Peter Richardson,
Zoo's reputation as an award winning innovative
contemporary architectural practice has recently been
established in Scotland. The practice aims to be
recognised in Europe for producing high quality design.
The office employs 7 staff all under the age 35 years
old. Zoo specialises in providing architectural,
environmental and urban regeneration service in a broad
range of sectors, but especially in the arts, residential
and leisure industries and have particular skills in
working with local communities. Zoo has a commitment
to the links between Educational and Architecture and
operate a mentor/pupil scheme in the studio, all staff
members are given the opportunity to become involved
in teaching at some stage of their development.

Fab Park. Millenium Space

Dimensions: 32.000 sq.m
Client: Hawthorn Housing Co-operative
Place of construction: Possil, Glasgow, Scotland
Date of completion: 1999

Regeneration: the project creates a new public space
in Possil that contributes to its regeneration by providing a range of spaces for all age groups whilst offering the local community a new focus, identity space.

Invitation: the workshop aspiration was to create new public spaces for Glasgow neighbourhoods
combing art, architecture and landscape architecture
of the highest quality. The concept provided an opportunity for Housing Associations to develop peripheral
areas with hight standards of urban transformation.

Development: the project was developed in
close consultation with the client board member. Two
models were made of the proposals to help explain
the design process. Zoo organised events to create
community awareness and support. A presentation
was made to the local primary school of computer
generated 3D images which were easily interpreted by the school children familiar with computer
game imagery. The same slides and projected on
to a screen at night, inviting the local community
to partecipate in the event. Workshops involving the
artist with groups of local children included a ques-
tionnaire which gave the design team additional information as to how space could be developed.

Description: the perimeter of the site is defined by a channel which drains the site and its steel
mesh cover deters dogs from entering and is a surface barrier to playing children. Within this rectangle the site is divided into two parts: hard and soft
with a ramped route between. The ramped route
between landscaped areas reinforces the original

track through the derelict site between the housing
and the local shop. Retaining walls are constructed using gabion baskets to create changes in level
and concrete interlocking walls, typically used at the
side of motorways. The hard landscaped concrete
surface offers an area for cycling and skateboard-
ing. The surface steps towards the corner and is broken into geometric planes of colour and texture.

The soft landscaped area is contour modelled
exploiting the sites change in levels creating profiled sculpted edges and forming sound buffers to
the neighbouring houses. In this landscaped area
is contour modelled exploiting the sites change in
levels creating profiled sculpted edges and forming
sound buffers to the neighbouring houses. In this
landscaped area are two play basins - the first forming a designed toddlers play area, the second a play
area for older children. A canopy structure on the
corner, opposite the local shop offers shelter and acts
as a focal point for the site. Play elements included a steel skate ramp, a graffiti wall, climbing wall
and a basketball hoop.

Artworks: text and images of encyclopaedic
information are shotblasted and inscribed in the surface of the concrete. David Shirigley, artist wished
to create a space full of information. The rules of
spelling and grammar are sited next to the graffiti
wall. He also created two 3D pieces, a sculpture
of a stone head is inserted among the rocks in the
gabion baskets and a monumental pair of stone feet
sit on a plinth.

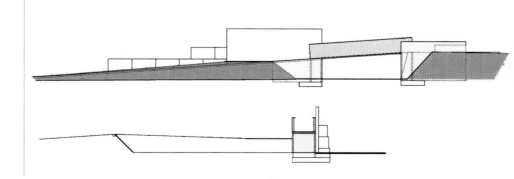

The main views

The art work
of David Shirigley

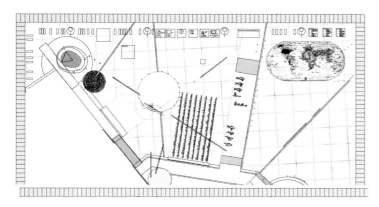

The main floor

Reason

How and where architects work is as important as what they build. Which is not to put technique ahead of content. Peter Richardson, founder partner of the Glasgow based practise, Zoo architects has a distinctive and determined approach to design. His work is uncompromisingly at the edge of the architectural debate. But he is also determined to communicate the energy and conviction of his work to the widest possible audience, and more importantly, to involve them in it. As part of Glasgow's Festival of Architecture in 1999, Zoo Architects were involved with the creation of one of a number of public spaces in the disadvantaged areas of the city. Zoo built a public space in Easterhouse, one of Glasgow's most troubled neighbourhoods – poor housing built in the 1930's, with heavy unemployment rates, a lot of crime, drug addiction and single parent families. Richardson sold his vision of a public focus for a trouble community, involving landscaping, artists, designers and architecture. He listened to what the community had to say, and integrated into his project, which became as much theirs, as his. The result is a striking urban intervention in a city on the brink of despair, that has provided a new focus.
Deyan Sudjic

Afterword

The Borromini International Architecture Prize is structured in two sections: the Borromini Prize and the Borromini Prize Youth Section.

The two sections, though united by common aims, address two different spheres: the first, that of established professionals, and therefore the experiences of players of clear international renown; the second, the research, experimentation and creations of young architects.

For both sections, the conferring of the Prize derives from a complex procedure for determining the candidates.

The complexity of the process is mainly associated with the desire to guarantee a broad-based comparison between architects coming from different geographical areas of the world and not necessarily already known on the international scene.

Deriving from this is the decision to work mainly using the Internet site www.premioborromini.org, on which all the nominations and candidacies are stored.

The individualised method has bring architects of clear value of different nationalities to the attention of the public visiting the site.

In order to guarantee the maximum depth of this research, the Prize has set up specific bodies that have performed important roles to arrive at the candidacies proposed.

First, a Committee was formed to promote the Prize, composed of specialists in the sector, critics, Italian architects and researchers active at international level with the task of facilitating contacts with institutions and personalities from the panorama of culture and architecture. The Committee's first task was to identify a group of 30 Nominators.

The Nominators were chosen on the basis to their qualities as illustrious personality in the international cultural panorama, sensitive to the values of the Prize and interested in seeking experiences that can express their motivations. Another important criterion was that of representing, with this group of personalities, the main geographical areas of the world.

The Nominators had the task of identifying, in the panorama of contemporary architecture, the works considered worthy of the Prize. The identified Nominators, who collaborated with the Prize, are: Stan Allen (USA), Anand Bhatt (India), Marco Brizzi (Italy), Jacqueline Burckhardt (Switzerland), Richard Burdett, (UK), Alberto Campo-Baeza (Spain), Cynthia C. Davidson (USA), Miha Desman (Slovenia), Akram El Magdoub (Egypt), Didier Fiuza Faustino (Portugal), Kristin Feireiss (Netherlands), Manuel Gausa (Spain), David Greene (UK), Ross Jenner (New Zealand), Bart Lootsma (Netherlands), Detlef Mertins (Canada), Yves Nacher (France), Kyong Park (USA), Didier Rebois (France), Livio Sacchi (Italy), Camilo Salazar (Colombia), Yorgos Simeoforodis (Greece), Dietmar Steiner (Austria), Deyan Sudjic (UK), Hiroyuki Suzuki (Japan), Klas Tham (Sweden), Marcos Tognon (Brazil), Martin Tschanz (Switzerland), Franco Zagari (Italy), Mirko Zardini (Italy).

Borromini Prize - Youth Section

The organisation of the Borromini Prize Youth Section has been conceived in four different phases: registration in the archive of proposals, identification of candidates, drawing up the short-list of ten, choice of the winner.

Self-candidatures

In an initial phase of the Prize, the possibility was given to young architects and/or groups of architects, who were not yet 41 years of age, to send their own candidatures to participate in the Prize. The regulations for participation envisaged the self-candidatures having to present, by 31 December 2000, a completed work, through 5 photos, a text describing the work and a brief profile of the author or authors. The works participating in the archive of Proposals of the Youth Section were 55; this is the list, by names of the works:

– Alternative to What – Normalgroup
– Area Cimatti – Alessandro Bucci

– Municipal Kindergarten – Beniamino Servino
– Auditorium Outside – noncon:form
– Blur Style – R&Sie.D/B:L François Roche
– University Campus – 5+1 architetti associati
– Shed 14 – Jean-Philippe Lanoire, Sophie Courrian
– Capua Chapel – Andrea Sciolari
– Casa Faniglia in Cuneo – Flavio Bruna and Paolo Mellano
– Casa Gioia – T-studio
– Casa Levis – Studio UdA – Architect Davide Volpe
– Casa Romolo Nardi – fgpstudio
– Stop Line Entertainment Centre – Marco Casamonti
– Pablo Neruda Centre – Extralarge
– Church of Urubo – Jae Cha
– Colombian Pavilion for EXPO – Daniel Bonilla
– SS.Giusto Parish Complex in Donato – Andrea Stipa
– Two Walkways for the Daikanyama District – BlueOfficeArchitecture
– Duke's – Nemesi studio
– Residential Buildings in Via Nervesa – Luca Mangoni
– Euskalduna Jauregia – S&Aa Federico Soriano
– Financial Centre Credit Suisse – Park
– Hanging Gardens in Venice – Daniela Moderini, Laura Zampieri
– Il Lazzaretto in Cagliari – Andrea de Eccher
– RACOTEK srl Laboratories – Giovanni Vaccarini
– LCI-Erudict Head Office, Groot-Bijgaarden – Martine De Maeseneer
– Mente-la-menta? – studio I-LAND
– Metal Dolphins – Alter studio
– Meta-Morphic – Cesare Battelli and Claudia Bonollo
– Varatella Pier – Marco Ciarlo
– New Piazza Mazzini – Stanislao Fierro
– Urban kitchen gardens – studio @@@
– Colombia Coffee Pavilion – Leonardo Alvarez
– Variable Message Panel – Fiorenza Asta
– Recreation Park for Children at la Villette, Paris – Isabelle Devin & Catherine Rannou
PC House – Team
– Covered Swimming-pool – studio di'-zain
– Scientific Museum Pole – n! studio
– Pedestrian Bridge in Marcheno – Camillo Botticini
– Prototypes – amgod#n
– Quintess Residence: Wave-Topos – Jang Yoon Gyoo

– RAN 310 – Manuele Balducci
– Reconstruction of a Japanese Garden – Péter Kis
– Restaurant Georges, Centre Pompidou Paris – Jakob & MacFarlane
– Restaurant in Treviso – Studio Workshop
– Restructuring of the former Hotel Newcastle – Studio Martucci – Oneto & Asoc.
– Restructuring for civil housing – Dellapiana Paolo – Francesco Bermond des Ambrois
– Tyre Retail – Camendzin Grafensteiner
– School of Architecture and Design – Castañeda – Hernandez – Rodriguez – Valencia
– Sixty Minute Man – Casagrande & Rintala
– Socialoft (twenty low-cost dwellings) – Alfonso Cendron
– Springtecture H – Suhei Endo
– Villa Azzurra Sanitary Structure – Davide Cristofani and Gabriele Lelli
– Condominium Villa – Alfonso Cendron
– You Make Me Feel Mighty Real – Fat

In this first phase, therefore, the response came primarily from Italy; these are the data on where the works were from:

Italy, 34 proposals
Europe (excluding Italy), 13 proposals
Americas, 6 proposals
Asia, 2 proposals

The Candidates
In this section the Nominators had the task of drawing up the candidates for the Prize for the Youth Section. Having studied the archive of Proposals, they then sent three candidates' names at most to the Prize organisation, one of which obligatorily taken from the aforementioned Archive. The new material that reached the Prize organisation was clearly the same that had been requested in the first phase of the Prize, accompanied by a text of justification on the work proposed. These are the 46 candidate architects and/or groups of architects in alphabetical order:

– 5+1 –University Campus in the former Bligny Barracks
– David Adjaye – Casa Elektra
– Jesús Mª Aparicio Guisado – Building with Flats
– Archea –Stop Line Entertainment Centre
– Architectural Office Casagrande & Rintala – Sixty Minute Man
– Architectural Research Office – US Armed Forces Recruitment Centre

– Atelier van Lieshout – AVL-Ville
– Anna Barbara, Rachaporn Choochuey, Stefano Mirti, Akihiro Otsuka, Luca Poncellini, Andrea Volpe – PC-House
– BlueOfficeArchitecture – Mei-Bashi (light bridge)-An-Bashi (dark bridge)
– Daniel Bonilla – Pavilion of Colombia – Expo 2000
– Alessandro Bucci –Cimatti Area
– CamenzindGrafensteiner AG – Tyre Centre/Art Gallery
– Javier Hernando Castañeda Acero, Luis Guillermo Hernández Vásquez, Carlos Mario Rodríguez Osorio, Mauricio Alberto Valencia Correa – School of Architecture and Design (Pontificia Università Bolivariana)
– Alfonso Cendron – Condominium Villa (ten low-cost dwellings)
– Jae Cha – Church in Urubo, Bolivia
– Davide Cristofani, Gabriele Lelli –Specialist Centre for Mental Illnesses, Villa Azzurra
– Design Office – Design Office 2
– Isabelle Devin, Catherine Rannou – The Garden of the Dunes and Winds
– DRMM – Moshi Moshi Brighton
– Peter Ebner – House for Students
– Shuhei Endo – Springtecture H
– Field Consultants – The Cottage Holyoake
– Toni Gironès – Passanelles
– Marco Graber – Thomas Pulver –Professional Institute, Berne
– Grego & Smolenicky Architektur – Accenture (formerly Andersen Consulting)
– Jakob + MacFarlane – Restaurant Georges, Centre Georges Pompidou
– Bernard Khoury – B018
– Mathias Klotz – School of Altamira
– Jean-Philippe Lanoire, Sophie Courrian – Restructuring of Shed 14 in Bordeaux
– Greg Lynn –Korean Presbyterian Church
– M&T, Müller & Truniger – Municipality of Jona
– Mathew & Ghosh Architects – White Walls and Light (House for Mary Mathew)
– Njiric + Njiric Arhitekti –Baumaxx Hypermarket
– Ocean North – The Intencities Pavilion
– Alfredo Paya Benedito –University Museum of Alicante
– Po.D – Instant Ego
– S&Aa – Euskaldina Jauregia (Auditorium and Conference Centre)
– Sadar Vuga Arhitekti – Building for the Offices of the Chamber of Commerce and Industry
– Zoe Samourkas – Apartment in Palaio Psychico

– Stéphane Schurdi-Levraud – Maison Combes
– Studio dd1479 – Hanging Gardens in Venice
– Studio R&Sie.D/B:L – Blur Style –Indistinct Style in the City and in the Country
– Kerstin Thompson – House on the Western Coast
– Vehovar&Jauslin Architektur – Restructuring of a Stairway and an Office in Wohlen
– Choi Wook – Studio Ilsan (for a Sculptor)
– Zoo Architects – Fab Park. Millennium Space

In this second phase, the geographical origins were different and of considerable interest:

Italy, 7 candidates
Europe (excluding Italy), 26 candidates
Americas, 7 candidates
Asia, 4 candidates
Australia, 2 candidates

Drawing Up the Short-list
The Jury was formed around certain international personalities from the world of architecture, plus a graphic designer, as an element not from inside the discipline, but close to it and capable of offering an external contribution. Initially the Jury was composed of:

– Domenico Cecchini, Councillor, Municipality of Rome
– Shigeru Ban, Architect, Japan
– Francesco Dal Co, Architect, Italy
– Javier Mariscal, Graphic Designer, Spain
– Carme Pinos, Architect, Spain

Subsequently, for institutional reasons, the Jury was made us as follows:

– Carme Pinos, Architect, Spain, Chair of the Jury
– Shigeru Ban, Architect, Japan
– Francesco Cellini, Architect, Italy
– Francesco Dal Co, Architect, Italy
– Javier Mariscal, Graphic Designer, Spain

The outcome of the first meeting of the jury was the drafting of the short-list of the ten finalists who were to contend for the first prize:

– Aro Architectural Research Office – US Armed Forces Recruitment Centre
– CamenzindGrafensteiner Ag – Tyre Centre/Art Gallery

– Jae Cha – Church in Urubo, Bolivia
– Peter Ebner – House for Students
– Shuhei Endo – Springtecture H
– Jakob + Macfarlane – Restaurant Georges, Centre Georges Pompidou
– Bernard Khoury – B018
– Mathias Klotz – School in Altamira
– Jean-Philippe Lanoire, Sophie Courrian – Restructuring of Shed 14 in Bordeaux
– Alfredo Paya Benedito –University Museum in Alicante

These are the new data, divided in terms of geographical origins:

No Italian

Europe, 5 candidates
Americas, 3 candidates
Asia, 2 candidates

On 15 June 2001 the members of the jury gathered at 10:30 and, after a discussion that took place in a harmonious atmosphere, as can also be gleaned from the attached minutes, they unanimously decided to declare architect Mathias Klotz (Chile) the winner, for the school building in Altamira.

They also decided to award a Mention of Honour to architect Bernard Khoury (Lebanon) for the building denominated B018 in Beirut.

What are the most significant
architectural experiments emerging on
the international scene? Who are their
authors and what sort of language are
they using? What are the themes of
design that are destined to take on more
and more importance? What parts of the
world are going to play a more central
role?
This selection of fifty works designed
and built by fifty young architects, all of
them under forty, sets out to present a
significant cross section of the research
under way in various parts of the world
and at the same time offer some
interesting reflections on what it means
to be an architect today.
The works presented have been chosen
from among those entered for the
International "Borromini" Prize for
Architecture and its section for young
architects. Fifty works selected by some
of the most eminent critics of art and
contemporary architecture; fifty works
described and commented on by their
authors and by the selectors; fifty
accounts of architecture in which text
and image combine in a daring attempt
to explain what it is to practice
architecture today.

ISBN 88-8491-140-0

9 788884 911407

£ 19.95 $ 29.95